D0569404

Loveworks

How the world's top marketers make emotional
connections to win in the marketplace

Brian Sheehan

powerHouse Books
Brooklyn, NY

♥

·····················

"When dealing with people, let us remember we are not dealing with creatures of logic.

·····················

We are dealing with creatures of emotion."

·····················

Dale Carnegie

·····················

Contents

*This book
is dedicated to
inspirational players
I encountered in
Saatchi & Saatchi
offices, and the
offices of their
clients, worldwide.*

♥

Case Stories

Kevin Roberts

CEO WORLDWIDE SAATCHI & SAATCHI

Fear drove me to create Lovemarks.

I had been a brand marketer for 30 years when I became CEO Worldwide of Saatchi & Saatchi and I saw that brands had become commoditized. Parity had invaded all elements of the marketing mix: price, design, quality, distribution, service, you name it. Excellence had become ubiquitous. Communications focused on performance, benefits, attributes. I saw growth curves becoming incremental; premiums eroding; products which were irreplaceable— but not irresistible. Technology had melted the event horizon and "new" had become "now"; consumer choices were becoming instantaneous, instinctive, intuitive. Above all, I saw that brands were serving corporations, the makers and marketers, and not consumers, the choosers and users. The question that formed in my mind was: "what comes after brands?" The theory was: ask a big enough question, and you might get a big enough answer.

In my years working with traders, retailers, in stores and souks, and directly with consumers, I had always felt the emotional qualities of a relationship were paramount. Trust and respect are essential but not enough; factors that we were to discover, such as mystery, sensuality, and intimacy, are at the heart of emotional connections.

And so Lovemarks was born.

Revolution starts with language and for us at Saatchi & Saatchi our world turned on this single word, this singular idea that brands could aspire to a higher order. Momentum turned into a movement: 250,000 books in print in 18 languages; dozens of academic papers; a brace of research studies; hundreds of conference speeches; hundreds of client campaigns; thousands of consumer stories coming into our website; magazine cover stories all over the world; a ten-part documentary series in China.

There was some resistance, shock, cynicism, and even outrage when the "L-word" was mentioned. My universal experience is that Lovemarks is an idea that people get at the first utterance. It has changed the way our clients view the marketplace. In yesteryear, marketing communications used to be about how impressive you were. Today it is about creating "priceless value" by answering the single question consumers have on their lips: "How are you going to improve my life?" Lovemarks helps us frame the conversations we have and the solutions we offer.

Brian Sheehan is the right person to be carrying this Lovemarks light fandango further down the road. He was a Saatchi & Saatchi ideas-man for 25 years, joining our New York agency right out of college and then taking on CEO roles in Japan, Australia, and at our Team One agency in Los Angeles where, among other achievements, he helped take Lexus to the number one position among luxury cars in America. I knew about Brian's passion for education and when he came to see me in 2007 and told me he was taking a teaching position at America's premier communications school at Syracuse University, I gave my full support believing that our journey together was unlikely to end there.

Loveworks is not only evidence of his scholarship and storytelling, but also of the contributions by Saatchi & Saatchi people and clients and consumers who have helped build, validate, and perpetuate this idea. I especially acknowledge the partnership with powerHouse Books, gutsy independent publishers of Brooklyn, New York, who in our time together have survived eviction, fire, hurricane, and the tumult of the book publishing industry. This is our sixth book with Daniel Power and Craig Cohen and the relationship has been one of the sweetest I can imagine.

Lovemarks is a journey that continues to evolve, especially as social media and the participation economy grows into the fabric of every society. I believe that the role of business is to make the world a better place for everyone. Lovemarks is an idea that takes us further by creating brands that give purpose and sustenance to the life of business, and to the business of life.

Brian's book shows how.

Kevin Roberts

This book has one purpose.

It is to provide tangible proof that when brands engage consumers' deepest emotions—instead of just appealing to their intellects, or even their basest instincts—they win in the marketplace. These brands win because their customers don't just respect them: they love them.

A cynic would say this is marketing sleight-of-hand, that people are paying more or buying more because of manufacturer image that adds no value in itself. On the contrary, the stories in this book will show that the brands that create the strongest emotional engagement provide tremendous value to their consumers. They provide empathy, understanding, inspiration, shared values, and education, among many other emotional benefits. And, they invariably provide great products, usually the best products in the market.

These brands do no less than improve the lives of their consumers via a powerful combination of superior product and emotional engagement. They are rewarded for this with higher sales, higher prices, and the most valuable market currency of all: the benefit of the doubt when they make a mistake. These special brands are called Lovemarks.

This book is built on the foundation of the book *Lovemarks: the future beyond brands* by Kevin Roberts, CEO Worldwide of Saatchi & Saatchi, published in 2004. That book had a big impact on marketing and advertising. But it has not been without controversy. According to Martin Bihl, erstwhile book review editor at *Advertising Age*, *Lovemarks* is still "one of the most polarizing books in modern advertising." Many people love it for revealing what seems obvious and just as many deride it for apparently stating the obvious.

Lovemarks

Mystery
Sensuality
Intimacy

Regardless of which side of the fence people are on, Bihl reminds us that *Lovemarks* clearly identifies the central question you will always have to ask yourself when you are working on an ad, a campaign, a strategy, a whatever.

"Will this make someone fall in love with this brand?"

....

When the *Lovemarks* book came out, Facebook was still a Harvard-based social network called "Thefacebook." A lot has changed since then. Kevin Roberts talked about Lovemarks creating "Loyalty Beyond Reason." In a digital world, where trying to create "advocates" for your brand is now second nature, Lovemarks seems, if anything, to have been ahead of its time.

The goal here is not to cheerlead, but to prove. In chapter one, we will review the basic precepts of Lovemarks theory. We will also review quantitative support for the value they create. Together, they are persuasive, but prove little conclusively. One can always argue with theory and especially with research statistics.

The cases in the following chapters will prove a lot however. We will see real world application and hard results. We will see how some of the world's greatest marketers, including Procter & Gamble, General Mills, Diageo, Toyota, and InBev, and brands including Pampers, Guinness, Lenovo, and T-Mobile have used deep emotional connections to build their businesses in markets throughout the world. In each case, the agency behind the campaigns was Saatchi & Saatchi, a company with 6,000 people whose stated focus is...

"To fill the world with Lovemarks."

....

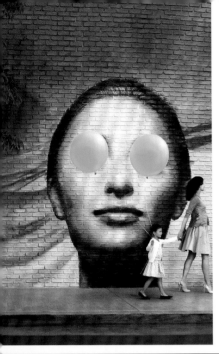

Case Stories

Following a summary of the key principles of Lovemarks theory, 20 case stories will be presented highlighting how some of the world's most successful brands have created Lovemarks of their own.

Photo: Ackerman + Gruber

Happy.

Could you hurt someone
who has your blood
running through their veins?

♥

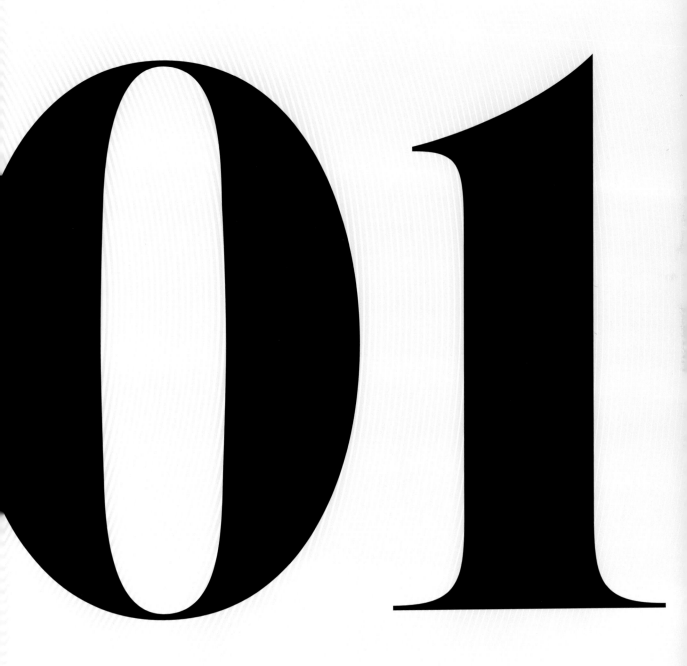

Lovemarks

01

This chapter is a brief review of the
fundamentals of Lovemarks theory, the tools
it supplies, and the research that supports it.
It is partnered with a short case story about
Procter & Gamble's Swiffer brand. Swiffer
took one of Lovemarks' key tenets and
brought it to life in a compelling way.

THEORY

Lovemarks Redux

Lovemarks theory is based on a simple premise: human beings are powered by emotion, not by reason.

This is the essence of the Lovemarks argument. If you want people to take action—whether for something momentous, like voting for a president, or seemingly mundane, like buying one brand of facial tissues over another—you need to appeal to their emotions.

Neurologist Donald Calne perhaps said it best:

"The essential difference between emotion and reason is that emotion leads to action while reason leads to conclusions."

How can we create the kind of appeal that makes people feel inspired or laugh or cry? First, we must realize that brands don't just get it by asking. They start by giving love, demonstrating that they love the people who buy them. The sea change comes when brands stop thinking about their customers as "them" and start thinking about "us." When marketers make this change, they start rewarding their customers every day with brand experiences that have special resonance in three key areas: mystery, sensuality, and intimacy.

Of all the potential aspects of emotional resonance, perhaps none is more important than the sense of mystery that comes from great storytelling. Annette Simmons, an expert in storytelling, puts it precisely: "When you tell a story that touches me, you give me the gift of human attention—the kind that connects me to you, that touches my heart and makes me feel more alive."

Mystery
is:

- Great Stories
- Past, Present, and Future
- Tapping into Dreams
- Myths and Icons
- Inspiration

Sensuality
activates:

- Sight
- Sound
- Smell
- Touch
- Taste

Intimacy
shows:

- Commitment
- Empathy
- Passion

Stories have huge value in business as well. They look in the right direction: at people. You cannot tell a story without characters and emotion and sensory detail. Even the dumbest chicken-crossing-the-road jokes have it. And stories capture us faster than the most elaborately produced annual report.

Sensuality is another aspect of emotional engagement that too many brands ignore. Lovemarks ask, "What does our brand smell like, taste like, look like, sound like, and feel like?" These are not easy questions, but the best brands find answers. If they are not in the food or perfume business, most marketers don't immediately think that taste or smell are relevant. But taste and smell are surefire ways to stretch your brain about your brand. Walk through any mall in America and you can smell Hollister from a mile away (you can hear it at a slightly shorter distance), it is also the only store that actually invades the corridor space with its red-tiled porch. Hollister gets sensuality.

"When you think about it, love is based on inspiration. We are inspired by brands for the same reason we're inspired by the people we love, because they have principles and treat me like a human being who is intelligent and has feelings. They show empathy and bring joy to my life."

Juan Carlos Rodriguez
Executive Creative Director
Badillo Nazca Saatchi & Saatchi

THEORY

The Love/Respect Axis

How do you know when you have gotten there?

Lovemarks are not created overnight. Marketers need to know where they stand in the beginning, and how well they are doing along the way to building a Lovemark. To help them, Kevin Roberts created the "Love/Respect Axis."

This tool allows companies to measure how much consumers respect their brands versus how much they love them. Low respect and low love? You are a commodity. Low respect and high love? You are probably a fad. High respect and low love? You are a solid brand with a big opportunity. High respect and high love? You are a Lovemark.

Call it Lovemarks or call it something else, but the pressing question for 21st-century marketers in a digital world of social networking and brand advocacy is how to engage people so they embrace and proselytize your brand. The answer to that question: move from the top left hand quadrant to the top right.

Lovemarks theory makes intuitive sense, but how do we know it really works? Well, that's what this book is all about. I will show how it works every day for some of the best marketers and brands that have a laser focus on building strong emotional connections with their consumers.

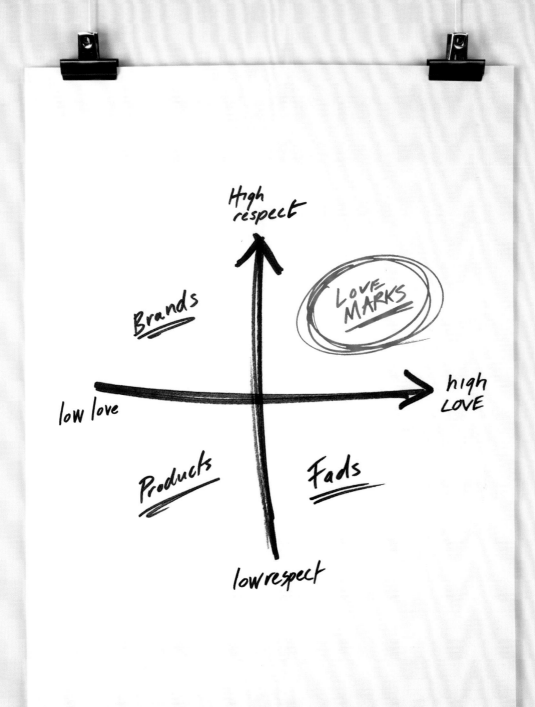

High
respect

Brands

low love → high
LOVE

LOVE
MARKS

Products   Fads

low respect

THEORY

The Data

First, let's look at some research statistics.

Knowing the need to prove the Lovemarks theory, Saatchi & Saatchi engaged pioneers in emotional research, London-based QiQ International. It was essential to have evidence showing that being a Lovemark delivered higher return on investment (ROI).

QiQ's work showed that growing love and respect can increase buying intention for a product by as much as seven times. Even if your brand has high respect already, you can double volume by increasing love and becoming a Lovemark. For example, in the cereal category, a respected brand can increase the probability of future purchase intention by 60% by increasing their love quotient. In the car category it is 133%!

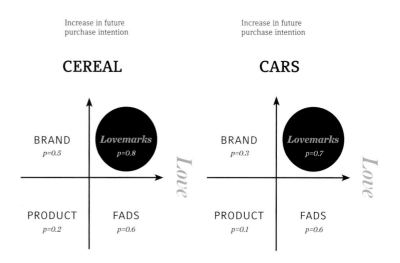

p = Increase in future purchase intention

Beyond purchase intention, people use their Lovemarks more often than they use other products. The average consumer uses their respected brands 26 days per year on average. For Lovemarks it is 119 days.

Frequency of usage (days per year)

Further research has supported the overall thesis. The 2007 "Firms of Endearment" study by Sisodia, Wolfe, and Sheth of 35 public companies that had Lovemarks characteristics showed an ROI of 1025% (between 1996 and 2006)—compared to only 122% for the S&P 500, and 316% for the companies profiled in Jim Collins' book *Good to Great*.

Love equates very strongly with loyalty. A survey of 60,000 shoppers across 50 markets found that if a brand can increase its loyal shopper base by just 5%, it can expect an increase in sales of 10%. And in this age of online social networking, loyal shoppers have a much higher propensity to recommend products to friends. In effect, people who love and talk about your brand online are now part of your sales force.

Research never sleeps. An associate company of Saatchi & Saatchi, AMR Research of London, has a reservoir of knowledge about what makes a Lovemark, after doing proprietary research on 4,000 brands in 50 countries and reviewing over 100 industries. It found that consumers are tough, awarding Lovemark status to less than 10% of brands surveyed.

Perhaps this is why Lovemarks don't just create typical loyalty. They often create loyalty beyond reason. What that means is that people who love those products often buy them without cross shopping any other brands. For example, in research, when they are asked if they can imagine a world without that brand, they honestly answer "no."

A recent paper in the *Journal of Marketing* by researchers Batra, Ahuvia, and Bagozzi (2011) reported on a three-stage study of brand love. The results of the study summarize Lovemarks in a nutshell. They found that when consumers feel a sense of love for a brand they have a higher sense of brand loyalty, spread positive word-of mouth, and resist negative information about that brand.

So, those are the basics of Lovemarks, and the thinking and research data behind it. Sounds good so far. Let's see how it works for brands trying to turn the theory into reality.

Swiffer Gets in "Touch"

In 1999, Procter & Gamble (P&G) created a new category—the "Quick Clean" category—with Swiffer. The Swiffer Sweeper offered an alternative to traditional mops for wet floor cleaning, brooms for dry floor cleaning, and feather dusters for dusting. Swiffer became a big success.

Over 10 years, it grew to annual sales over half a billion dollars. Swiffer's legion of fans loved the ease and the effectiveness of the product. But by 2011, sales were beginning to stagnate, in large part because it was increasingly hard to convince consumers who had not already adopted Swiffer.

The underlying problem was that many consumers found it hard to understand how the product—which came in a small rectangular box on the shelf and required assembly—could do the same thing as their trusty mops, brooms, and dusters, only better.

Swiffer's traditional box

The key to success was to understand the power of a Lovemarks principle: sensuality, more specifically the sense of touch. Of all the senses associated with love and loyalty beyond reason, being able to touch and be touched can evoke some of the strongest emotions. Shoppers want to be able to touch the product they are going to buy, especially when it relates to taking care of their family and cleaning their home. The box packaging prevented many shoppers from making a tactile and emotional connection to Swiffer. They couldn't really imagine how it would work. This was the product's biggest barrier to new trial.

Saatchi & Saatchi X in Springdale, Arkansas, handles P&G's shopper marketing program with America's largest retailer, Walmart. Together, the three companies worked to find a solution. They were a potent combination. Over the past few years, some of the most innovative and inspiring work in shopper marketing has resulted when these three put their heads together.

What they came up with for Swiffer was an "out of the box" solution. In other words, they planned on making the product available in its final assembled form instead of a small box.

We've made it easier to find a better clean.

But it wasn't going to be easy. Shipping the product as a preassembled stick was much more difficult. And displaying the product would take a complete redesign of the retail aisle.

P&G solved the packaging and shipping issues. Saatchi X solved the display issues and put together an engaging multimedia communications plan. Walmart prepared to execute it in-store. By 2011, after testing each aspect of this new approach, Swiffer was ready to get in touch with a whole new group of potential users in a big way.

The product was now available in an aisle that had been completely redesigned around Swiffer's new preassembled sticks, and color-coded to differentiate Swiffer's varied products. The advertising campaign was also a joint effort. Many of the communications carried both Swiffer and Walmart branding. The effort included print ads, circular ads, online banner ads that showed the product bursting out of its pack, and commercials highlighting the new Swiffer section—"redesigned with you in mind"—on Walmart's in-store TVs.

Swiffer also scored a coup by announcing the redesigned Quick Clean aisle on an episode of the popular daytime talk show, *The View*. The show was perfectly targeted at Swiffer's core female target, many of whom watched the show when they were cleaning the house.

To help convert interest into trial, the new packages had overt messaging about Swiffer's money-back guarantee under the theme "Put Your Money Where Your Mop Is." According to Doug Van Andel, global creative director at Saatchi X, "Emphasizing the money-back promise, which is standard business practice for both P&G and Walmart, added fuel and significance to the more tactile product and the aisle redesign." Now there was simply no reason not to try it for the first time!

The new packaging and communications improved the clarity of Swiffer. It made the brand more intuitive. It allowed shoppers to understand which specific Swiffer product they needed, in a split second rather than a minute or two. This helped change shoppers into buyers.

Out of the Box Equals Off of the Shelf

The P&G, Saatchi X, Walmart triumvirate grew the Quick Clean category at Walmart by nearly double the rest of the category growth at other retailers.

Swiffer's package transformation and the re-invention of the Quick Clean category has become a testament to the power of great shopper marketing. It has been cited by the *Wall Street Journal* and the campaign won both gold and silver Effie awards for shopper marketing. It is a literal example of thinking outside the box.

Swiffer's success is a testament to the power of dialing up love by making products more sensual.

Xploring 02

This chapter features case stories for Guinness and UNICEF. The common ground for these stories is their creative use of research. Both brands eschewed the kinds of research that is done in false environments, like focus group facilities. Instead, they used a proprietary type of ethnographic research that Saatchi & Saatchi calls "Xploring." Xploring gets to the truth of how people really behave versus what they say they do.

GUINNESS **brings out the Power in you!**

Guinness: Africa Falls in Love

The year is 2003. In the city of Douala, in the West African nation of Cameroon, a motorcade is on the move.

A good-looking, slim, and athletically built black man is sitting atop an open 4X4 as thousands of people line the street waving and cheering. Young men and burly security guards sprint alongside the car in the sweltering heat and dust.

Is he a political leader, a world famous singer, an African soccer hero? No. Is he a famous actor? Sort of. His name is Cleveland Mitchell and he plays a character named Michael Power, whose job is to help Guinness sell beer—actually beer's darker and heartier cousin, stout.

In order to understand this phenomenon, and the magnitude of what Guinness has achieved in terms of an emotional connection with its drinkers from 2003 right up to today, we need to look back over a decade. In fact, we need to look all the way back to 1998, when the character named Michael Power was born.

Guinness' Challenge

By 1998 the Guinness brand was already well known in Africa. The product sold there was Guinness Foreign Extra Stout, a slightly stronger and more bitter brew than the Guinness stout drunk in some other parts of the world.

It was respected by many. It was even similar in color and bitterness to many traditional African tonics. The Guinness brand's challenge was to significantly increase sales by transforming respect for the product into love.

Specifically, Guinness wanted to double sales in Africa by 2005.

The agency for the Guinness brand in Africa is a combination of Saatchi & Saatchi's London office (where the strategic planning is done) and Saatchi & Saatchi's South Africa office (where the creative is developed). The Guinness brand's advertising runs in a number of African markets, where local Saatchi agencies also provide support. The biggest markets are Nigeria, Ghana, Cameroon, and Kenya. The smaller markets include Ivory Coast, Gabon, Benin, Togo, Uganda, Tanzania, and Burkina Faso. However, Nigeria is the biggest market by far.

To set the stage, it is important to know what life in countries like Nigeria was like in 1998 and to a large degree even today. There is the obvious. Nigeria has the largest population in Africa at over 160 million people. It is an economically challenged country. Its per capita income is below $3,000 and many people earn less than $2 per day. A bottle of Guinness sells for 40% of that, or 80 cents. Back in 1998, Nigeria's infrastructure was inchoate. Very few people had televisions, and access to any kind of entertainment content was scant. Few African men were icons in film or television.

Against this backdrop, the Guinness team decided to do something positive to inspire consumers. They introduced two big thoughts in their advertising. The first was that there is "greatness" inherent in Africa, in general, and within African men in particular. The greatness and quality of black men parallels the greatness and quality of the world's most famous black beer. The second thought was even more inspirational. For Africa and its men to succeed, they needed to "believe" in their greatness. These combined thoughts, as executed in its marketing programs, have driven the brand's success for the last 13 years.

It may even be reasonably suggested that the Guinness brand has actually helped inspire the men of Africa to better lives. That might sound like marketing malarkey, but as we will see, it is not an unrealistic claim.

The Michael Power Campaign

Step one in Guinness' approach was the introduction of "The Action Adventures of Michael Power." Michael Power was in essence an African James Bond. Commercials featured Bond-like evil geniuses, boat chases, and plane explosions. Michael Power rescued innocents in peril, got out of the tightest of tight places, and always came out on top, with a bottle of Guinness never too far away.

On an entertainment-starved continent, Michael Power became a phenomenon. He was an icon of African cool, but more importantly a role model who communicated that African men could be admired and could achieve greatness too. As Graham Cruikshanks, Saatchi & Saatchi South Africa's deputy managing director, put it:

"Michael Power became the quintessential man of Africa, a beacon of hope and inspiration to millions of people."

....

The commercial films were so popular that some African TV stations ran them as free programming. At the height of the campaign's popularity, Guinness produced a full-length Michael Power movie, called *Critical Assignment*. The film was shot in five African countries using only local actors and crew.

Michael Power: the James Bond of Africa

The movie was wildly popular in Africa. It was also distributed in the rest of the world. It opened the New York African Film Festival at The Lincoln Center, and it won the Jury Prize for best feature film at the Hollywood Black Film Festival. The film, which focused on the world's water crisis, also gained endorsement from the United Nations Environment Program (UNEP) and carried the UNEP logo.

The Michael Power campaign ran for seven years from 1998 to 2005, which is a long time for a single campaign. Brand awareness in key countries reached 95%. Michael Power's awareness stood at 93% across the continent (versus 98% for Nelson Mandela). Awareness for the movie alone, in Nigeria for example, was 89%. In Ghana it was 81%.

The Guinness marketing team has a research measure that is akin to measuring love (i.e., "What percent of people adore the brand"). After the movie ran, adoration increased by 22%, to 61% of Nigerians surveyed. Those who adored the brand were more numerous than all other groups combined.

Sales volume rose by leaps and bounds. Guinness doubled its sales in Africa by 2003, two years ahead of schedule.

"Reach for

Where to From Here?

How do you follow success on this level? Could Guinness possibly drive emotional engagement even higher in the years to come? Unbelievably, the answer was yes. Guinness was about to create an even more powerful campaign.

One way Saatchi & Saatchi helped Guinness figure out what the next step should be was to conduct "Xploring" research. Xploring is Saatchi's trademarked name for a special type of qualitative research it has pioneered. It has proven extremely effective for the agency and its clients for uncovering meaningful consumer insights, especially in developing markets. In 2006, Saatchi published a book about their insights from Xploring in the world's biggest developing market: China. It was called *One in a Billion*.

Unlike the standard focus groups or one-on-one interviews, which usually take place in false environments like research facilities or shopping malls, Xploring is a type of research commonly called "ethnography," where researchers get actively involved in observing people in their real day-to-day lives. Unlike most ethnography, however, Xploring starts with no preconceived notions or structured questionnaires. Its goal is to go deep into a country and the psyches of the people who live there—which in developing countries often means putting on backpacks and hiking boots.

The ultimate objective of Xploring is not to answer predetermined—and therefore leading—questions, but to provide intimate portraits and stories that snap a picture of the country's typical consumers into sharp focus. Xploring emphasizes the authentic, the immediate, and the emotional. It allows consumers to tell their own stories. In Africa, the fortitude needed to do this properly was extreme. Not only is the continent vast, but lack of infrastructure meant that Xplorers needed to be hearty, tenacious, and deeply dedicated. According to Charlie Finnigan, Saatchi's lead planner on the Guinness account, "Over the years, our Xploring trips have involved talking to everyone from panel beaters, market traders, and factory workers to politicians, tribal chiefs, university lecturers, writers, and Nollywood [Nigerian Film Industry] film directors."

But it is worth it. As Graham Cruikshanks said:

"A huge amount of our creative understanding comes from Xploring. It invariably leads us to something interesting and compelling, and enhances the creative process."

greatness"

A Drop of Greatness in Every Man

The Xplorers found out that life in Africa was invariably tough, but that people drew inspiration from anything that signaled their ability to rise above their circumstances and make more of their lives. This source of inspiration was combined with an insatiable optimism in Africa and an unwavering belief that success could be around any corner. In fact, every single person at Guinness and Saatchi & Saatchi who was interviewed for this story expressed that they were inspired, quite personally, by the incredibly positive spirit of the African people and cultures they encountered in their Xploring research.

These key research findings reinforced the dual communications foci of "greatness" and "believe," but they pushed them in a new direction. Previously they had been wrapped in a fictional character as a source of idolized inspiration—a catalyst behind renewed momentum and crucial at the early point of the brand's evolution. Now they would be focused on real African men who achieve greatness by improving their lives and the lives of their communities every day. Greatness would no longer be about Michael Power; it would be about the "Drop of Greatness in Every [African] Man." Guinness was a great beer for great men, and the brand exhorted every man to "Reach for Greatness."

The campaign came to life in 2006 with a commercial about a man named "Udeme," who realized his dream to become a pilot. The commercial was narrated by his close friend.

He tells us:

....

"My friend Udeme is a great man. When he was a boy, his teacher asked him where he dreamed of working. 'There,' he said...

[as the narrator looks up to the sky],

and he was good to his dream. He knew that if there was one thing we have a lot of it is sky, big, beautiful sky. In the whole of Africa, he couldn't think of a better place to work..."

....

Visually, the shots of Udeme flying his small plane are a celebration of the beautiful vastness that is Africa. And he is not just flying for fun: he is making deliveries of crucial supplies to people in remote areas. He comes home to meet his friends in the local bar. As he tips his bottle, he likes to say, "Let the beer see the sky, but not for too long."

What kind of impact did this softer, more personal approach to greatness have? "Udeme" was voted one of Nigeria's all-time favorite commercials. More importantly, the commercial became a staple of popular culture, entering the vernacular in myriad ways. "Udeme" has become a nickname for Guinness. Patrons often say, "I'll have an Udeme please!" It is also common to hear drinkers toast by saying,

"Let the beer see the sky."

John Pallant, Saatchi's executive creative director for Europe, Middle East, and Africa, believes the commercial was an excellent example of the mystery, sensuality, and intimacy that are cornerstones of Lovemarks:

"Mystery in the sense that these characters have depth, and there is a real sense that they have lives beyond the commercial, about which we are intrigued to know more. Sensuality in the very rich production values, a celebration of the spectacular beauty of Africa—its landscapes and its music. And intimacy in its understanding of what is important to African men, and the resonance of the language."

{ This film won a D&AD Silver award in the film craft category. }

Udeme in his airplane
delivering vital supplies

This commercial was followed by the story of a European football [soccer] scout traveling across the continent looking for talent. As the scout is driven through cities and remote villages, the quality of the play he sees is astounding. He tells the viewer that he "was expecting to see greatness, just not so much of it."

It is difficult to do justice to Africa's passion for football. In much of Africa, football is more than a sport; it is closer to a religion.

This commercial was not just a fictional story thought up by an agency creative team. It came specifically from an Xploring exercise. In an interview, over a beer, one of the coaching staff from the Nigerian national football team told the Saatchi team how they find new players: "Sometimes you travel to the smallest villages and find world class talent playing on gravel pitches, under trees…." The commercial felt authentic in other ways too. It featured a host of well-known East and West African football players, and it was shot with the help of renowned football choreographer Mike Delaney. In short, it showed how many real African men had lifted themselves up from humble beginnings to greatness.

The latest ad in this series debuted in 2011. It is perhaps the most subtle and meaningful story in the campaign. It is the story of two brothers. The elder brother has made a name for himself in the city and is now returning to the village for a visit. The younger man clearly admires what his brother has achieved. He begins to narrate the story by saying:

Femi arrives back at his village and meets his younger brother

"My older brother Femi is more than a man…."

Throughout the commercial we see Femi living up to his younger brother's accolades. After Femi arrives back in his village and distributes the customary gifts, the two brothers sit, sharing a Guinness. Femi challenges his younger brother, saying: "A boy dreams but a man does. Brother, are you ready to drink at the table of men?" He proudly offers a bus ticket to the city. It is time for the younger brother to follow in the footsteps of the older brother.

Like the ads before it, this commercial strikes deep into the hearts of African men. The campaign understands a culture where fathers, brothers, tribal chiefs, priests, and other grown men share a strong social responsibility to improve the futures of their younger sons, brothers, and brethren. It challenges those who have lifted themselves up to do good for their villages, tribes, and families. It also challenges younger men to reach for greatness within themselves.

As John Pallant noted,

"The strength of this commercial is that it doesn't feel like advertising; it feels like a story about two real people."

....

This commercial was shot in Nigeria, which brought many production challenges. Aside from flying the production crew in from all over the world and having to deal with the logistical issues created by moving a big team into remote areas, the team weathered torrential rain, 18-hour shooting days, and even interference from the "river gods."

According to some of the local actors and villagers, the river gods preferred they only do a single take [shot] of one of the commercial's scenes. This kind of authenticity shines through in the spot and the whole campaign. In fact, much of the dialogue was derived from actual observed consumer conversations, how they talk about Guinness and how they express the transition from being a young man to becoming a responsible adult: a "real man."

Femi challenges his younger brother to follow in his footsteps

On the back of this new campaign, since May, 2010, "brand health," based on Guinness' tracking studies is the strongest it has been in four years, and many of the brand health measures are at all-time highs. According to one research report, "Guinness is [now] seen as acting as an empowerment brand, and a confirmation of Nigerian manhood." The most impressive measure, however, is sales. Nigeria is now one of the top three Guinness markets in the world.

You've got

Reaching greatness is not just about advertising.

Ruairi Twomey, an Irishman who was recently Diageo's Head of Marketing & Innovation for the Nigeria Hub (note: Diageo is Guinness' parent company), tells the tale of how Guinness leveraged the brand and Nigeria's belief in itself to make the seemingly impossible possible.

Twomey was put in charge of the Guinness brand Africa in 2010. Aside from being instrumental in approving the "Two Brothers" script, Twomey challenged his team to find ways to get African consumers to "fall in love" with the Guinness brand all over again. He attributes his focus on love as the core strategy to having read Kevin Roberts' *Lovemarks* cover-to-cover one night soon after he arrived to take over marketing in Nigeria. He gave the book to his team. As he put it: "Our job was to get people to love the liquid, the brand, and most importantly the brand's values… A brand that people really love believes in its consumers as much as they believe in it… For Guinness to be a Lovemark, it needs to take risks. It needs to invest and believe in its drinkers, or it is just another beer." So Twomey and his team took one of the biggest risks of all.

As we have already seen, Nigerians love football even more than they love beer, but Nigeria was only #42 in the international rankings. One of the perennial top teams in the world was Argentina, and Argentina had often spoiled Nigeria's World Cup hopes. It was a team that Nigeria had never beaten. So the Guinness marketing team came up with "Guinness: The Match"; a quest to fulfill every Nigerian football fan's dreams. They were going to invite Argentina to come to Africa for the first time to play a select Nigerian national team ("The Super Eagles") on home soil.

The list of problems was almost endless. How to convince Argentina? They had little to gain by winning and a lot to lose. Nigeria was also in the middle of a presidential election that might have led to widespread social unrest. Add to this almost no preparation time to organize a major event. And what if Nigeria were humiliated? How would people feel then? Would they still love Guinness?

As Twomey admitted, "On paper, there was no chance we could pull it off." But the Guinness team had a pithy response to doubters with lists of problems. They said, "You've got to believe." To the Nigerian people and their national team, they were saying that the Guinness brand believes in you, so you need to believe in yourselves. And if we all believe, greatness can and will be achieved: nothing is impossible. What Twomey also knew was that his team was consistently excellent in planning and execution. This would be no thrown-together program, but a deliberate, professional marketing program done on a short timetable.

"Guinness: The Match" pitted
Nigeria against mighty Argentina

to believe

The game took place on June 1, 2011. Nigeria beat Argentina 4–1. The Vice President of Nigeria handed out the medals to the winning players.

The Guinness brand team even found ways for the people of Nigeria to get into the game. Everyday people were drafted as assistant coaches and official photographers. Many others were asked to sing the national anthem on the giant screens in the stadium in front of the 42 million people who were watching the match on TV. The match was televised in seven countries.

The amount of love, respect, and trust African consumers share with the Guinness brand is truly astounding. Beyond TV commercials and events, the brand has a program they call Guinness VIP, which is a mobile phone community that provides such things as social chat, football content, and updates. Much of Africa has adopted mobile phones as the primary means of communication, leapfrogging more expensive technology like laptops. In Nigeria, for example, there are over 90 million mobile phones for a population over 160 million. That puts them in the top 10 for mobile penetration worldwide. Computers, and even televisions, have far less penetration than cell phones.

How popular is Guinness VIP? It has become one of Africa's premier social networking platforms. Over 8,000 people are on it at any given time, and over 1.2 million people every week. It is, in fact, the continent of Africa's largest mobile phone community.

In Nigeria more people are talking to Guinness—and to each other through Guinness—than Facebook has users in Kenya. In a country where infrastructure can be very spotty, millions of people trust Guinness for communicating with each other more than they trust their national telecoms.

In short, the Guinness brand is finely in tune with the hopes, dreams, and aspirations of African men. The brand earns their love and admiration because it first loves and admires them. Perhaps most importantly, it inspires young African men to reach for greatness and to believe in themselves, their people, their families, and their culture.

In a 2012 research report to gauge feedback on its most recent advertising, consumers gave the following responses:

"It touches on the core of African society."

"It defines what Africa is."

"It's speaking to me because that is what we do."

"It is challenging me that I should do the same thing: it is a wake up call to me."

The brand has perhaps even helped make life better in Nigeria, and other countries in Africa, by inspiring their young men to live better lives. That is saying quite a lot for a pint of beer.

UNICEF Gets to Know China

In 2006, Saatchi & Saatchi started its greatest Xploring challenge ever by covering 50,000 kilometers in China with backpacks and sneakers. Sandy Thompson, Saatchi's previous head of planning worldwide, was instrumental in the creation and definition of Xploring. As she said at the time, "To Xplore, you need to have the courage to approach strangers and ask dumb questions. You need to realize that statistics mean nothing and that you know nothing. An Xplorer needs to be fearless."

Here's how she described the story of how Xploring led to a breakthrough for UNICEF in China as told in the book *One in a Billion*:

"UNICEF is a fantastic organization that makes a real difference in the lives of thousands of children in need of healthcare and education. Like many of our clients, UNICEF came to us with the story of what they had achieved so far. If they were to continue making a real difference they needed to gain awareness not only with the public at large, but also with the Chinese government.

"The typical ad for UNICEF would include needy children, a few scenes of kids in a classroom, kids being fed, and kids receiving medical attention. All of this was good, but we knew it would not meet UNICEF's objective of raising awareness further.

"Our idea came one day when we were walking in the streets of Wuhan. A young girl selling roses approached me for money. You should never give money to street kids, but as I was missing my own children, I instinctively reached for the loose change in my pocket. Within seconds I was surrounded by 15 or 20 children, clinging to my clothes and pleading for money.

"Our van's driver instantly began shooing them away. He picked up stones and started throwing them at the kids. They were around the same age as my children and the driver's children. He and I had spent hours talking about our families, yet he was treating these children like animals.

Someone else's child will supply food to your family

Someone else's child will take you to work everyday

Someone else's child will protect you from danger

"This situation helped us realize that we could not make a difference for UNICEF unless we helped people think about children differently. While we all love our own children, we are often ambivalent to other people's kids, and in particular needy kids. If UNICEF was going to be a success, they needed people to realize that, every day, someone else's child has an impact on their life.

"We produced a commercial for UNICEF using as much stock footage as we could. For the first 20 seconds there is not a single child in the commercial: just adults. We reminded the viewer that these adults are all other people's children, and that they have had an impact on our lives every day."

The commercial was very successful. It was shown more than 3,000 times at prime time on over 300 Chinese TV stations, all at minimal cost to the client. It won the gold at the Asian Marketing Awards, a Gold Pencil at One Show, and it received extensive coverage in the region on multiple communication programs.

♥

People Power 03

This chapter features case stories for Toyota Camry and SKOL beer. The common ground for these stories is how they have unleashed the power and emotions of the people who use these products. Both brands have a refined sense of what makes their customers tick, their feelings and values. Most importantly, they have used that understanding to ignite people's passions, enabling them to take an active role in celebrating the brand for themselves and others.

CAMRY CASE STORY

Camry and the Power of Personal Stories

Mark Turner is not easily daunted. An Englishman transplanted to Los Angeles, Turner is the chief strategy officer at Saatchi & Saatchi LA. He has led the team developing strategic plans for Toyota's 15-plus car and truck lines for the better part of a decade.

Before that, he was the planning director on the Lincoln-Mercury account at Young & Rubicam. You could say, where cars are concerned, he has seen it all.

That was before 2010 however. That year started a period more difficult than Toyota had ever seen. On the heels of a tenacious recession, Toyota was hit with a massive recall, which in itself led to the equivalent of $2 billion in negative publicity over just two months. (Note: The value of publicity, positive or negative, is measured by comparing the media space the messages received to the cost of buying that space based on advertising rates.) Then 2010 gave way to 2011, which brought an earthquake in Japan, a resultant tsunami, and a nuclear scare. Toyota's image issues were now compounded by vehicle supply issues. As a result, Toyota lost the confidence of many consumers and the equivalent of over five years of previous sales growth.

Turner and his team had their work cut out.

Nowhere was there a bigger concern for Toyota's recovery than for the Toyota Camry. Camry is Toyota's best-selling car. In fact, for more than a decade it has been the best-selling car in all of America. Toyota and Saatchi LA had worked relentlessly, year after year, to first establish Camry as America's favorite car and then to keep it there. To a degree, as goes Camry, so goes Toyota.

On the plus side of the ledger, Camry had unquestionably been a Lovemark for many Americans for a very long time. It had built up a tremendous amount of goodwill as evidenced by the fact that over 40% of all people who buy a Camry go on to buy another one—the usual figure for non-luxury cars is less than 6%. On the minus side, the confidence Camry owners had in the car, and the brand, had been very badly shaken. Based on recent history, automotive nameplates that had suffered similar impacts, like Audi in the 1980s or Ford's Explorer in the 1990s, had taken 10–15 years to recover.

Toyota Camry has been America's best-selling car since ads like this one ran over a decade ago

In the midst of this turmoil, Tim Morrison, who was Toyota's corporate manager of marketing communications at the time, felt there was a silver lining: "We knew the negative things our drivers were hearing was not at all what they were experiencing in reality."

The launch of the 2012 Camry had a lot riding on it. Toyota, Saatchi, news stories, and automotive analysts saw Camry as a linchpin for a Toyota comeback. The team would leave no stone unturned to tap into the emotions of Camry buyers to try to reignite the trust, the respect, and the love. As Turner said, "We believed our recovery rate was directly linked to the power of Camry to reclaim its Lovemark status. There were eight solid competitors in the mid-sized sedan market, all with similar features and benefits. We needed to win on emotion."

Research, Research, and More Research

Step one was to conduct what the team calls "Consumer Context Research" or CCR. This is innovative ethnographic research focused on the media behavior of a selected audience. The goal is to observe not only all of media the audience interacts with on a daily basis, but also to determine which of those interactions are most meaningful. As Evan Ferrari, director of strategic planning at Saatchi LA put it, "A person may be at home watching *The Oprah Show*, but if they have it on in the background while they are doing household chores, and only really pay attention when something rare and unique happens—like Tom Cruise jumping up and down on Oprah's couch—then that is not necessarily a meaningful interaction, even if that person watches it every day."

The results of CCR give a precise profile of how different audiences use media to fulfill their needs. For the slightly more upscale buyers of the Toyota Highlander sports utility vehicle, for example, the media they use when they get home from their stressful jobs helps them unwind and relax. They prefer warm and fuzzy programming to action programs or news. The planning team says that CCR helps the advertising "hit the sweet spot," providing the right emotional pitch for each piece of communication, whether the consumer is sitting down with a glass of wine after a tough week to enjoy *People* magazine, revving up with a cop drama, or catching up on the day's news online.

Perhaps the most innovative part of the CCR process is how it informs the creative process. Years ago, media teams and creative teams had little interaction. With CCR, the creative teams are brought in at the earliest stages. They see a complete profile of the desired audience's media habits, which helps them come up with ideas that are not only on messaging strategy but which fit the media context that best speaks to the audience. Sometimes it helps them bend the media, or even create relevant new media platforms altogether.

Saatchi & Saatchi's logo for its proprietary Consumer Context Research

CONSUMER CONTEXT RESEARCH

Beyond CCR, the team used social listening on the web as a key research tool. They visited sites where their customers congregated and listened to what they had to say in online forums. They paid special attention to forums on the key third-party automotive sites where most people go to research cars as part of the buying process, sites like Edmonds.com and Kelly Blue Book. In addition, they interviewed hundreds of people in traditional focus groups, one-on-one interviews, and car clinics.

Getting Emotional with the Unemotional

What they learned from this exhaustive research process was almost as daunting as the challenge of reversing Camry's fortunes. They learned that Camry owners, on the surface, are not very emotional about their cars. In fact, they are intensely rational in their automotive purchase decisions. These are solid middle class Americans. Their car purchase is one of the biggest financial decisions they will make for their families. Getting it wrong is not an option. As Rebecca Lindland, automotive journalist for National Public Radio, noted when talking about Camry buyers: "God love 'em, but they're appliance buyers. They are not interested in making a statement on the road."

This was not necessarily a great starting point to rekindle brand love. Camry owners were dubbed "quiet competitors." They do an incredible amount of research about their cars before buying them. They want to make sure beyond a shadow of a doubt that they are getting the best product at the best price. Jerry Beers, another member of the Saatchi LA strategy team, told the story of how obsessively competitive these buyers can be:

"When we spoke to them individually, they would sometimes whisper, even though we were alone in the room, and say things like, 'Do you know what my neighbor paid for his car that doesn't have the engine power, gas economy, and features of my car?' They get a real rush from making a smarter purchase."

....

Beers told another story that highlights just how careful and conservative the decision process is for some Camry owners: "We were interviewing the wife of a Camry driver. She said they were on vacation and her husband had researched, planned out, and pre-booked every meal for the whole vacation. He discovered that he had neglected one meal when they got there. As they were walking around, his wife pointed to a restaurant and said, 'Why don't we try that place?' He said, 'What if it is bad?' His wife said, 'But honey, what if it is good?'" Clearly, Camry drivers don't like to leave things to chance.

Adding to the lack of emotion was the fact that Camry is in the largest, most competitive category in the industry: the mid-sized family car. In no other category are there more competitors. Because buyers of mid-sized cars are so practical, the whole category tends to be commodity-driven on features and price. Tapping into love and emotion was not going to be easy.

As the problems mounted, one of the biggest ones actually held the seed for the solution. But it would take the team some digging to figure out how. The answer was not necessarily in what Toyota had to say about Camry, but what other people did.

As seen in the CCR research, because Camry buyers do so much studying before purchasing, the third-party automotive research sites, enthusiast sites, and automotive forums are critically important in the purchase decision. What was most interesting, however, was that potential buyers were much more interested in the reviews of average people, rather than what any of the editors, experts, or automotive journalists had to say. They wanted to hear what people like them had to say about the cars, and wanted to read about other people's personal experiences with them. In fact, Turner's strategic planning group estimated that almost 60% of influence for buying a Camry came from reading the experiences of people the potential buyer has never met! It was not just that the sites were the most influential media touchpoints; it was that the stories of real people were the most influential purchase-motivating information.

For many car owners, the need to share stories leads to the creation of consumer-driven sites and forums dedicated to a particular model or brand. In fact, in an audit of the top 25 sites mentioning Camry, five were forums dedicated to other car brands.

So how many dedicated fan forums did Camry have on the web? Zero. Now remember, we are talking about the best-selling car in America with almost 7 million cars sold over 30 years, and over 4 million still on the road. And zero!

This was not necessarily a weakness of the Camry, but it gave an invaluable insight into Camry buyers. On one hand, the stories people told about their cars were the biggest potential influence on Camry buyers, yet Camry buyers, in general, were reticent to tell their own stories. When the team thought about it, it made a lot of sense. Camry drivers are not exhibitionists. As we have seen, they like to whisper their love for Camry; it's a secret.

What was really exciting was that when Camry owners were compelled to tell their story, as they were in focus groups, a remarkable thing happened: one Camry story led to another. In these stories, a car that the automotive journalists likened to vanilla ice cream sounded more like a vanilla sundae with sprinkles, strawberries, and M&Ms on top. The people telling the stories got excited and emotional, and the stories just got better and better. As Toyota's Morrison put it, "Once you got them talking, they didn't want to stop." Maybe these buyers were not just purely rational beings after all. Still waters ran very deep.

The challenge now was crystal clear for Toyota. Could they come up with a Camry campaign that would compel hesitant Camry owners to share their great stories with other Camry owners, and mid-sized family car intenders, who are surfing the internet in order to make an informed decision?

In effect, Toyota and Saatchi wanted Camry owners to give a "review" of their car online. The challenge was stated internally as:

"Let's make Camry the most reviewed car on the planet."

The Camry Effect

The answer Saatchi LA offered was to create an online forum, called "The Camry Effect," where Camry owners could share their stories. They would be provoked through a major multimedia campaign including television and various dynamic online ads. The Camry Effect was even featured in Super Bowl ads. One of the most innovative ads featured a tie-in with the Shazam mobile phone application, which allowed people to have their mobile phones listen to the music on the commercial while it was playing and link them directly to the Camry Effect site.

Once people got to the site, it was much more than a boring storytelling forum. It was a dynamic social site that used a series of questions, adapting to each individual's answers, to make the site unique to each person. It allowed people to customize their stories by timeline or location or theme. It gave visitors hundreds of 3D and handmade illustrations and visuals to help them make their story one-of-a-kind.

The Camry Effect website helped generate about 100,000 stories

In the end, each user was able to create a personalized, seamlessly animated, 3D experience that was unique to them. It was also dynamic and changed day-by-day, giving people a good reason to go back again.

It would be logical to ask how a site that is intended to inspire existing Camry owners to tell their stories would be effective in getting non-Camry owners to participate. The website was just the start. The stories it created became the content for an advocacy-based advertising campaign, on the web and in traditional media, intended to change opinions of non-owners and create leads. The team described it as a "Yelp-like experience for Camry," referring to one of the web's most popular socially-driven user review sites. How engaging was the campaign? Did it get the taciturn Camry demographic to open up?

After its launch, there were 13,000 stories. After the Super Bowl advertising, the number jumped to 88,000 stories in just a few days. Today, there are almost 100,000 stories on the website (including one from this author, who is in love with his 2009 Camry Hybrid).

One of the most common story subjects is the durability and longevity of Camrys. During their research, Toyota and Saatchi took the unusual step of putting both Camry loyalists and Camry resisters into a focus group together. The one thing they all agreed on was that Camrys last a long time.

According to Bob Zeinstra, Toyota's national advertising & strategic planning manager, who has been involved and approved the campaign every step of the way, "Stories from second owners talking about how much they love their Camry are common, as are stories of the cars being passed from father to son, mother to daughter, and even three generations."

These stories are critical because they are both dripping with the emotion of family ties and driving home a key rational point that is primary for this customer: Camrys keep going and going. Passing the car down to your children is a defining act that combines durability and safety, the most important purchase criteria in the category. A keen sense of a brand's past, present, and future is also one of the defining characteristics of a Lovemark.

Romeo Sandoval told the story
of his tricked-out Camry

One special story of Camry longevity came from Chris Newell, who inherited his 1997 Camry from his grandfather. He traveled across the United States from the East Coast to Los Angeles. In a short film on the site, we hear how the Camry is a surrogate for his departed grandfather, who drove the car until he was in his mid-80s. Chris tells us that his grandfather is with him in spirit, reminding him of the simple road trips the two used to take together.

Another owner's story goes like this: "Little did I know when buying my Camry in 1994 that a few years later, I would adopt a little girl born in 1994, and now many years later that girl born in 1994 is driving my 1994 Camry. She's 17, but the Camry has 235,000 miles on it."

Not every story is about how long a Camry lasts. Romeo Sandoval astounds us with the jacked-up Camry he has specially tuned with a passion. There is even a story about a kid named Cameron because he was born in a Camry.

Toyota's Zeinstra says the campaign has the earmarks of an "equity asset," an idea that goes beyond a short-term campaign and becomes core to the brand over a significant period of time. For the 2013 Camry, Toyota is already planning to extend the idea, including a series of documentaries about Camry owners and their stories by the Academy Award-winning director Errol Morris.

What strikes Zeinstra the most about the Camry Effect is that potential storytellers needed to answer a survey of at least eight questions on the site, share their stories worldwide, and let the site tap into their Facebook and Google privacy rights. By design, this was not a super-simple exercise. Toyota wanted the experience to be immersive and the stories to be considered, yet almost 100,000 people went through the process: people who were supposed to be quiet, conservative, and non-emotional as related to cars.

The campaign went beyond advertising and became a dealer-prospecting tool. An application was created so dealers could show potential customers reviews and stories from Camry owners who lived in their own neighborhood, or even their own block.

The Effect of the Camry Effect

The results of the Camry Effect campaign have been nothing short of inspiring.

- The campaign will soon pass 100,000 stories, which was Toyota's stretch goal for this quietly competitive consumer group.

- 14.4 million people chose to watch the Camry Effect spot online leading up to and after the Super Bowl.

- Camry has received over 460 million unpaid media impressions to date.

- Engagement on the site during Super Bowl week was an average of over four minutes per visitor.

- Image measures for Camry are up and nowhere is this more pronounced than on Camry's image for "Lasts a Long Time," which has reached its highest level ever.

- New leads jumped by 19% and real-world interest in the car jumped 800%.

A key component of lead generation is what the auto industry calls "hand raisers." They are people who visit a site and ask to be contacted by a dealer for more information. The typical place for hand-raising is on a brand's main website, where there is everything from pictures to product demonstrations to pricing. Yet in the same seven-month period since the launch of Camry Effect the percentage of hand raisers was 148% higher on the Camry Effect site than Toyota.com.

Loyalty beyond reason is a gaudy claim, but Camry can prove it, perhaps better than any other product. Camry buyers are highly pragmatic. Yet, as we have already seen, when Camry owners buy a new car, over 40% of them buy a new Camry. That is loyalty. Loyalty beyond reason is demonstrated by the fact that about 45% of people who buy a Camry never cross-shop another vehicle. For Camry re-purchasers, the number is a whopping 60%!

For the world's most rational car buyers, if that is not loyalty beyond reason, then nothing is.

Loyalty Way Beyond Reason

A key aspect of creating loyalty has been to service the Camry community with "The Camry Effect." As Mark Turner likes to say, "This is a perfect manifestation of Toyota's overall philosophy in communications: humility, interest in the consumer, a focus on a better future for their drivers. In this case, there are millions of Camry owners who want to do my job for me, and I am inclined to let them."

The Camry Effect has played a major role in reestablishing Camry's Lovemark credentials. It reinforces key areas like intimacy (personal stories), sensuality (stories of power, luxuriousness, and comfort), and mystery (exhibiting loyalty beyond reason), and as we have already seen, a keen sense of past, present, and future. And Camry is still the best-selling car in the US.

SKOL Invades Carnival

Brazil's most popular beer had a breakthrough by encouraging their drinkers to take over Brazil's largest cultural event: Carnival. Like Toyota, they did this by reversing their communications.

Carnival celebrations in cities all across Brazil are legendary. Preparations take months of planning and effort. The competition to have the best party, the best dances, the best parade floats, and the best music is extreme. For the young partygoers, they plan for it as if it were a war consisting of a series of battles, albeit a very fun war. They need "plans of attack" for parties and attracting the opposite sex. Their preparations are done with "ultimate victory" in mind. So, SKOL took the war analogy to incredible heights to create something fun, engaging, and memorable.

It helps to have a little history. In 1996, SKOL was the number-three beer brand in Brazil. Working with F/Nazca Saatchi & Saatchi, they transformed the brand's image. SKOL was one of the lightest beers in the market, which might have been considered a weakness.

Instead, they positioned the brand around smoothness and the advertising idea of "Desce Redondo," which literally means "Goes Down Round." In Portuguese, this perfectly captured the smooth taste and led to some iconic advertising about the "roundness" of the flavor. Over time, roundness was also seen to extend to social circles of friends who drank together. SKOL soon shot to number one and gained a reputation for being young, irreverent, funny, and even a little subversive.

The brand's subversive side was on display with their 2011 campaign for Carnival called "Operation SKOL." The military-themed campaign was centered around the brand's fan page on Facebook and communicated across many media touchpoints, like television, print, internet, and outdoor. The Facebook application was a game where players needed to create troops, complete missions, and invite others to join in via their social networks. The goal was to have an army of SKOL drinkers take over parts of Carnival.

SKOL set up troop headquarters in strategic cities throughout Brazil. Working with promotional agency Bullet the best troops were invited to the Carnival celebrations and treated to their own troop airline, troop ship (a converted cruise ship), and even a hotel suite, called the "Love Bunker" to help them win their partying war. Guilherme Pasculli, who heads up planning on SKOL at F/Nazca Saatchi & Saatchi, put it this way:

"We provided the consumer and his friends with the possibility of attending Brazil's five top Carnival celebrations, traveling by private jet, Jeep, and ship. This was a previously unimaginable experience."

This wild building served as
SKOL's Carnival headquarters

Operation SKOL conquered the best Carnival celebrations by air, sea, and land. It also conquered television and internet coverage. According to Pasculli, "By putting our drinker at the center of the experience, our SKOL troops attracted media attention and placed us squarely in the category's top-of-mind." Despite not being the official sponsor of Carnival, SKOL was the most recalled brand after Carnival. The campaign's television commercial was also highly memorable, using the soundtrack of Aerosmith's "I Don't Want to Close My Eyes," but set to a distinctly Brazilian samba beat.

The level of viewership for the TV commercial was higher than the reach of the second and third largest TV channels in Brazil, combined. In the end, the brand gained a 4% market share increase nationwide, and a huge 14% increase year-over-year in the key Carnival cities during the promotion.

SKOL invaded Carnival
by air, sea, and land

SKOL's Carnival campaign was driven in large part by Facebook and social networks

The brand's Facebook fan base grew from 160,000 to 2.6 million in just three months, and peaked at 5 million, making it the largest beer fan page in Brazil. The game alone mobilized over half a million participants. SKOL broadcast various Carnival parades in key cities, over the internet, reaching 18 million viewers (live and on-demand).

These were outstanding results given the huge competitive spending that takes place during this time of year. "Developing SKOL projects during Carnival is always an enormous challenge," said Marcelo Penna, F/Nazca's client services director, "because we have to be relevant during a period in which domestic and regional brands use mass media to bombard their campaigns." In this environment, he noted, "Our multiplatform project increased share of mind and beer consumption."

SKOL had succeeded in turning around the focus of the communication, putting the drinker in the center, not the product. As a result, the brand became a medium for a greater experience in their lives. Jose Porto, planning director at F/Nazca put it this way: "The brand's objective was not to be an associated product, but rather, to be one of the 'band of brothers' in the Carnival celebration."

Pedro Earp is marketing director for SKOL at parent company InBev. He wants the brand to be much more than just a beer. As he put it, "SKOL's goal is to bring out the best of youth, anytime, anywhere." In Brazil, there could be no better opportunity to bring out the best of youth than Carnival. According to Earp, "Carnival is the period of the year that most represents SKOL's spirit and values."

SKOL continues to be the number one beer in Brazil and, despite only being sold in Brazil, is now the second-largest beer in InBev's global portfolio (after Bud Light). It has achieved that by understanding how to tap into the emotions of its drinkers. It has created loyalty beyond reason because the brand models the fun and irreverent attitudes of young adults in Brazil. It adds to that a clear product benefit of smooth taste that "goes down round," for you and your friends.

SKOL is now an undisputed Brazilian Lovemark, in general, not just in the beer category.

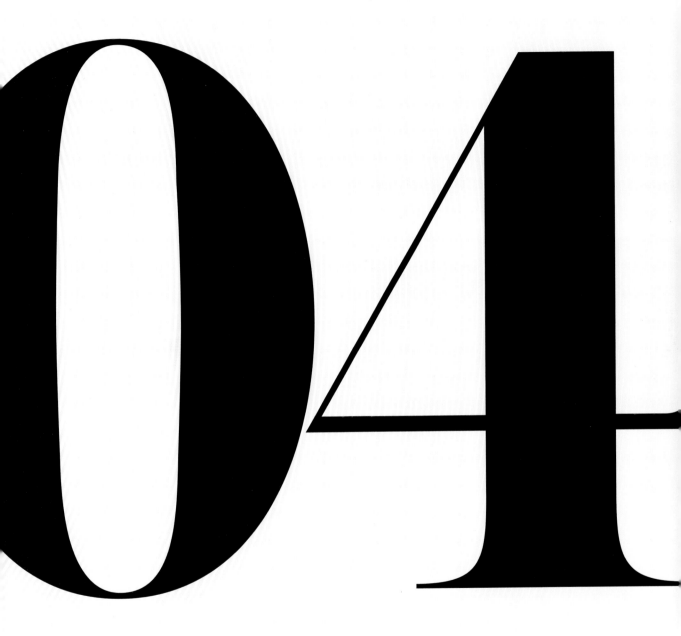

Tribes

04

This chapter features case stories for Pampers and Cheerios. The common ground for these stories is how they marshalled a wide array of creative resources in one place at one time with a sense of mission and focus. They did it by convening what Saatchi & Saatchi calls a "Tribe." In each case, the Tribe was able to deliver an inspirational creative idea that helped the brand connect better with existing and new customers. In doing so, it also helped each brand surmount significant marketing problems.

Photo: Ackerman + Gruber

PAMPERS CASE STORY

Pampers Performs a Miracle

"Whatever we can do to make life a little better for a baby, we will do." That is Jodi Allen's mantra.

In 2010, Jodi was Procter & Gamble's North American vice president and general manager for baby care. Making life a little better for babies had driven everything she and her team did every day for Pampers. But that year she and her team encountered a problem—a big problem.

It started with the launch of one of Pampers' most innovative products: Pampers DryMax diapers. On paper, this shaped up to be one of Pampers' most successful launches ever. The new diaper was 20% thinner and twice as absorbent as Pampers' regular diapers. They were the thinnest and driest diapers on the market. They spelled more comfort for babies: more comfort for wearing and more comfort from wetness.

Then something went wrong. A small but vocal group of moms started clamoring to bring back the old diapers. At first, they did not like the new design changes. Soon after, they claimed that the new diapers gave their children a significant burning diaper rash caused by chemicals in the Drymax diaper. By way of Pampers' Facebook site and a variety of social networking sites, the moms' accusations spread like wildfire across the globe. News stories began to pop up. Investigations were launched. Consumer advocacy groups were openly challenging Pampers.

Pampers had done extensive product testing before putting the product on the market. However, they took the complaints very seriously. These were moms talking. P&G went to extreme lengths to understand the concerns and to recheck the product's safety with both external and internal experts. During their detailed investigation, the Pampers team could not find a single baby who experienced skin safety issues, beyond normal levels of diaper rash, as a result of DryMax. In general, no diaper can guarantee one hundred percent that your baby will never get a diaper rash, and Pampers had never made that claim. In the end, the team was convinced by what they had learned that the Drymax product was perfectly safe.

But it did not matter.

Consumers were skeptical, and Pampers' reputation was on the line.

Cliff Francis and the Tribe members review hundreds of creative ideas they generated

Worst of all, many moms were questioning whether Pampers had the best interests of their child in mind. This was not the dream launch Jodi Allen and her team had envisioned.

They knew they had a better product, but they were losing the hard-earned trust of the moms who bought it. Trust was a particular issue with mothers of newborns—who are the lifeblood of the diaper business—because many were choosing a diaper for the first time.

The brand team knew they had never stopped working to make life better for babies. It was in their DNA. They had to find a way to make moms regain their trust in the brand. As Allen (a mother of four) said,

"If they just knew the people behind the brand. Babies are what we love. If we were doing anything to harm babies we would stop. On the flip side, if there was anything more we could do to help them, we would."

....

The Pampers Tribe

The Pampers brand had a black eye. It is P&G's biggest brand, and the pressure on client and agency to find a solution was tremendous. To help chart the way forward, P&G and Saatchi & Saatchi used one of their most potent tools, the "Tribe." A Tribe is Saatchi terminology for getting a diverse group of creative and strategic thinkers—often from different parts of the companies, or even outside the companies, and from around the world—to an offsite location for a few days to focus on a single big issue or opportunity. The diversity, isolation, and focus of such a team allows people to avoid getting caught up in daily distractions, and to focus on matching the core values of the brand to the needs of its consumers. In the case of Pampers, this group would allow the brand to refocus on what had made Pampers a Lovemark to begin with.

Deborah Mills, Saatchi's brand agency leader on Pampers, described the Tribe—which met in a downtown Manhattan hotel—as the collection of "an amazing group that really clicked—thinkers and creatives, brand people and non-brand people, clients and non-clients." Jodi Allen briefed the group and joined it at key junctures. The Tribe was moderated by Cliff Francis, Saatchi's worldwide creative director on P&G. Francis felt very confident about this group because it had the three elements that he believes lead to success:

- A good brief

- Motivated participants

- Open-minded clients who want great things

One thing Cliff and the team knew was that the answer would be something emotional. The brand had already done lots of rational communication to say that DryMax was safe, but the issue was trust, and trust is as deeply emotional as you can get.

The Tribe got to work and developed literally hundreds of communications ideas. Jodi Allen rejoined the group at the end of the first day and told them, "You haven't pushed it far enough." She knew instinctively that extraordinary circumstances call for extraordinary ideas. Now was no time to play it safe.

The team agreed and went back to work on day two to come up with something special. They realized that their job was really nothing more than communicating the values that Pampers had always lived by, its undying focus on the welfare of life's most special people: babies. Getting this right would remind moms why Pampers had been trusted for so long.

At the same time, the team was hoping to modernize the image of the brand. Research had shown that people characterized the brand as highly professional, but a little stiff and didactic, perhaps more like a competent nurse than a loving mother.

Pampers celebrates all babies...

Whether she's 3 months early

Where Miracles Come From

By the end of day two, the Tribe had landed on a simple yet powerful idea. It would not be an explanation of what Pampers was about; it would be a powerful and deeply considered point of view from the brand about how special babies are, no matter where they come from. It would be Pampers' DNA on film. It was called the "Miracles" campaign. That night, Cliff Francis took the idea and wrote it up as a manifesto to kick off day three.

The manifesto led to one of Pampers' most evocative campaigns. The core component of the campaign was a 60-second film that would run on YouTube and selected television programs. The film was a celebration of every kind of baby and every kind of family. It had a sensibility that was far removed from Pampers' stiff and somewhat formal image. It was contemporary and touching, and showed an honest love of babies—all babies. As Deborah Mills said later, "Every time we showed the film to a room full of people, there would be people crying."

Visually, the film reflected the truth of modern families by showing, for example, a teenage mom, a mom in her late forties, a pregnant woman in a wedding dress, and an embryo being fertilized in-vitro. It also showed all kinds of babies, like a premature baby, triplets, a Down's Syndrome baby, and a mixed-race baby. Concurrently, the words of Cliff's manifesto flashed across the screen:

Whether he is planned or not.

Whether she is 3 months early or 10 years late.

Whether he has a young mom or a surrogate.

Whether she is through IVF or adoption.

Whether she has special needs or a lot of needs.

Whether she learns one language or two.

Whether his family is close by or far away.

However it happens.

Pampers believes every baby is a little miracle...

To celebrate...support... and protect.

Pampers. For Every Little Miracle.

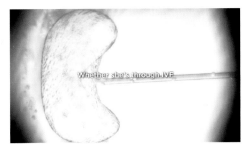

...no matter how they come into the world

Thank You Pampers

The team quickly realized they had something special. Aside from teary-eyed responses in internal meetings, YouTube views grew apace, reaching a total of over 1.7 million views. It soon became the most highly-viewed Pampers video online, ever. Discussions about the video started popping up all over the web, especially on mommy blogs and forums. As a result, Pampers gained 240,000 new Facebook members in just four months. Media picked up on the story, helping Pampers gain over 450 million media impressions. Twitter alone generated over 26 million impressions.

But the response went even deeper than the Pampers team could have imagined. Before long, Pampers starting receiving thank you letters, emails, and postings from parents who were representative of many distinct lifestyles and situations. They wanted to voice their appreciation for being recognized. Many of these parents felt under-served or ostracized by society, popular culture, and even brands. They found Pampers' affirmative message satisfying and liberating.

Here is an excerpt from one letter received:

"You see, my daughter has Down's Syndrome and this time last year I could not even say those five words let alone write them in a letter. I was suddenly a part of a community I knew nothing about…and never saw. I was becoming aware of the way that people looked at us when we were out and began to dread being 'outed'. People can be so tactless at times and even though I think that my daughter is beautiful, extra chromosome and all, it says a lot to open an email for a national campaign and see a little girl that looks like your baby. I thought, 'Someone thinks she's beautiful,' and felt the tears. So thank you P&G for caring enough for the DS community and for all other children born with special needs for putting one of our children front and center and not tucked away in a sidebar. Our children are beautiful. It speaks to the character of your company that you would debunk public perception and allow our 'normal' to be shown to the world."

There are times when commercial communications are elevated. When they actually matter. This was one of those times. Deborah Mills put it succinctly: "The film was seen by many as giving a voice to those who have been overlooked. Pampers was in tune with a new vision of what it meant to be an 'average' family." The film became a catalyst that changed the consumer dialogue from negative crisis reaction to positive baby welfare appreciation.

Pampers was back where it needed to be. It was a champion for newborns. As a result, sales and share increased, especially for the Swaddlers product for 0–6 month old babies and new moms, which went to all-time highs.

Positive online sentiment about the brand grew 300%. The campaign's highest return on investment (ROI) was in the social space. Brand scores for "trust" and "would recommend to a friend" went up sharply.

Steve Rothman, Saatchi's global planning director on Pampers, put it this way: "It's not just what you sell, it's also what you stand for. Moms reconnected with Pampers because we shared their values. We always had. We just had to remind them, vividly." This was the right balance for a company that consistently challenges itself to have the best product performance while staying true to its values for all of its brands in every category.

The impact of this campaign was felt throughout P&G. In their internal "People's Choice" award competition, as voted by the company's employees, the film won first place as the favorite ad of 2011. That was no small feat, since it was up against competition like the Cannes award-winning Old Spice campaign. John Brase, P&G's North American marketing director for baby care, said he had never been prouder to be part of a campaign. He went on to say: "'Miracles' transformed our organization. It has influenced everything we have done since as a brand-building community."

Top P&G executives, like Martin Riant, group president of global baby care, and Marc Pritchard, global brand building officer, brought the film with them on their global sojourns. They highlighted that Pampers had not just been solving a problem, but reasserting and redefining its roots and its core. As Pritchard put it, "The fruits are in the roots. When we connect the brand's passion to what consumers are passionate about, everybody wins." The fact that 2011 was Pampers' 50th anniversary was a perfect time to get in touch with the brand's roots, captured by the words, "50 years of Celebrating Miracles."

Miraculous Missions

A complement to the "Miracles" campaign is the "Missions" program. The program fosters consumer participation by encouraging people to pledge small acts of "celebrating, supporting, and protecting" newborns and parents. The idea is to pay-it-forward for new moms. An example of a pledge might be, "I pledge to make dinner for a new mom." Once participation thresholds are met, Pampers jumps in with a "miraculous response." Sometimes the response is broad, like a Groupon for social responsibility. Other times it is more personal. For instance, one miraculous response was a Mothers Day Event where Pampers threw 1,000 baby showers with gifts for moms who otherwise would not have had the means for such a celebration.

The "Miracles" film was integral to creating this online movement. The reaction of the mommy blogger behind "The Shopping Momma" is typical. She has a page dedicated to the Missions program. This is how it starts:

"I am so delighted to have a small part in the Pampers Miracles campaign. When you learn more about it—and watch the tear-jerker video below—I think you'll understand why. And, the good news is you can participate, too."

There is a tremendous lesson here. Even the best brands stumble and experience troubled times. If, like Pampers, they have strong values and never stop striving to do the right thing, they will emerge stronger than ever.

Jodi Allen said it best in the beginning:

"*Whatever we can do to make life a little better for a baby, we will do.*"

....

Jodi Allen attributes the campaign's success to something she has always told her children:

"If you have good values that you stand by, you can overcome any issues, crises, or problems that you need to face."

CHEERIOS CASE STORY

Cheerios Reclaims the High Ground

Another compelling example of a Tribe being used to refocus a Lovemark is Cheerios. Launched in 1941, Cheerios is an American icon. For decades, the brand has been one of America's best-selling cereals, and one of the best-selling products at parent company General Mills. For many, its yellow box evokes strong emotions and memories of family and childhood. It is a food that everyone from toddlers to adults has in common.

By 2011, the brand had been focused for some time on a dual strategy. One focus was on Cheerios being a great first finger-food for infants. The second, where the most effort was going, was its heart-health benefit, highlighting that the whole grain oats in Cheerios can help lower cholesterol. This was a great competitive point of difference, and the brand had been successful with the message. Over time, however, business growth began to slow. A brand that had had such a rich emotional heritage was being defined too narrowly on a functional health benefit. The big risk was that, over time, Cheerios might be seen by younger consumers as slightly medicinal, as opposed to heartwarming, fun, and tasty.

Thierry Ibri, Vice President of Marketing for Cheerios, summarized the situation as follows: "We were so focused on the specific needs of moms and baby boomers that the brand was playing smaller than it was in reality. The brand was bigger than that for consumers. We wanted to regain the love and get our mojo back."

The Saatchi & Saatchi team's first step was to get a grip on how consumers were feeling about the brand. They conducted social listening on the web, following relevant blogs and social media conversations to see what people were saying about the brand in their own words. According to Amy Martin, who was Saatchi's lead planner on the account, "What we heard was a lot of people talking about a million reasons why they loved this brand; and they were all emotional reasons." For example, one woman talked about how she moved home with her parents temporarily because her husband was transferred in his job. The first thing she saw when she went in the kitchen was the yellow Cheerios box and it made her feel instantly that everything was going to be okay.

"The Harvest" Tribe members arriving in a Minneapolis oat field

The team then pulled together a Tribe, which they nicknamed "The Harvest." It met for three days in a field 90 minutes south of Minneapolis, where some of Cheerios' oats were grown. The group included many people who had worked on Cheerios and others who had not. There were dozens of people involved, including agency creative teams, planners and account people, digital professionals from partner agency Zeus Jones, clients from General Mills, and public relations people. Despite the 100-degree temperatures in mid-summer, Martin referred to it as "a dream briefing, where a diverse team of some of our best minds put their heads together to come up with a breakthrough solution." The specific brief was simply stated:

"Give people a reason to love Cheerios again."

....

The Tribe focused on everything they knew about the consumer and the product itself. They were even briefed by an expert on oats, whom they took to calling "Handsome Jeff." They were blown away by Jeff's knowledge for the intricacies of the subject and his passion for it.

The idea that came out of the Tribe, interestingly enough, was connected closely to an idea that was created as initial stimulus for the Tribe. The Cheerios creative team had put some posters together to help set the mood for the meeting. One board featured the word "SMILE," in Cheerios' typeface, on the brand's distinctive yellow background. The "i" on the word "smile" was dotted by a Cheerio.

When the team saw the boards, they had a strong gut feeling that the core idea captured something true and important about the brand. Seeing a single word on a yellow background with a Cheerio for punctuation was incredibly simple and powerful. According to Peter Moore Smith, the creative director on Cheerios, and the man ultimately responsible for developing the campaign, "We came up with lots of great ideas in the Tribe. They were all about the hundreds of ways people eat and love Cheerios. The goal was to remind people about them as honestly as possible. We had to capture them simply and just get out of the way." Smith and the team realized their best creative executions married with the simple graphic words on yellow background were a magic combination.

The internal stimulus boards for the Tribe

The team took to calling the idea the "Simple Power" campaign. As Amy Martin said when discussing the ads, "You didn't know why you loved them; you just felt it emotionally. And that's what being a Lovemark is all about."

Thierry Ibri agreed. He felt the emotional connection. Importantly, he also realized that the idea had the potential to unify what had previously been two separate streams of messaging into a single stream that would appeal to boomers, moms, and just about everyone else who had ever eaten Cheerios.

Simple thoughts on a yellow background evoke strong emotions for Cheerios

Photos: Ackerman + Gruber

Eventually, "Simple Power" became a fully integrated campaign featuring a number of TV commercials, print ads, outdoor boards, digital banners, and a Facebook application.

One television commercial features a father in the kitchen in the morning with his young son, who is in a high chair. The father pours a pile of Cheerios onto the tray of the high chair. As he turns his back, an older brother seven or eight years old runs into the kitchen in his pajamas. He scoops the Cheerios from the toddler's tray into a bowl and runs away, while putting some in his mouth. The father turns around and says laughingly, "The Cheerio bandit got you again!" He and the toddler just smile. The spot ends with the words "Never Outgrown" and a Cheerio bouncing in to become the period. Another spot features a teenage girl with headphones on in her kitchen. She tosses individual Cheerios, one at a time, into the air, trying to catch them in her mouth, with occasional success. The spot ends with the yellow background and the word "Dinner," with a Cheerio dotting the *i*.

The commercials don't feel like they are acted or scripted. Instead, as Saatchi's management director Rodes Ponzer noted, "They feel like watching a movie of your life." The scenes are ordinary, even mundane moments. But they capture people's idiosyncrasies, and how deeply Cheerios has become ingrained into the lives of average Americans.

Similar to the Toyota Camry case earlier in this book, the team realized that the people who love the product are often the most articulate at expressing what makes it special. So, building on Saatchi's idea, Zeus Jones took the lead to develop a Facebook application called "In a Word, What Does Cheerios Mean to You?" The app allows people to summarize the brand in a word and share stories and pictures to make it come to life. As always, real people share things that surprise and delight. One entry equates Cheerios with "Love." It is accompanied by a picture of a bride and groom leaving their wedding ceremony and being showered not by rice, but by Cheerios. It also says, "This is how much we love Cheerios!"

The Simple Power campaign has helped Cheerios go from rational narrowcast to emotional broadcast.

"Simple Power"

Early Results

The campaign is in its early stages. So far, the reaction has been just what General Mills had hoped for. The outdoor boards, in particular, are getting strong emotional responses. During an in-market test of the outdoor, at America's largest mall—Mall of America in Bloomington, Minnesota—the team observed first-hand as people in the mall asked friends and family to take their pictures in front of the giant yellow billboards. According to Ibri, Cheerios is now receiving "unsolicited feedback every day from people telling them they love the campaign and including pictures of themselves in front of the billboards, which is amazing." The executions that seem to be sticking most are the ones with deep emotional resonance, like "Love" and "Smile."

The reaction in the blogosphere has been similar, as reflected in this recent blog post (on a legal blog no less):

"With its bright yellow background and black characteristic font, the billboard looks like a box of Cheerios made for Godzilla. And I loved it. This billboard instantly hit me with a wave of nostalgia, even stronger than the Minnesota heat wave we have been experiencing. Like most children, I was raised on Cheerios and learned to recognize the yellow box at a very young age. Those boxes contained my favorite breakfast food, and if I was lucky, a maze or word scramble on the back that I could solve while spooning down the crunchy o's. Later, I would use those same boxes to create a fort, surrounding myself with a yellow wall at the breakfast table to fend off my younger brother seated across from me.

"Now, as an attorney, I laugh to no one in particular when I realize that instead of a ® next to "Love," the word is accompanied by a small Cheerio. Touché, General Mills, touché."

Anecdotally, the campaign is working. During the next few months, hard data will follow to let its creators know if they have made a quantifiable and sustainable success.

One of the most important aspects of the early feedback is that the strongest emotions seem to be tied to the media that Cheerios has not historically used very much. It is a television-heavy brand, yet outdoor and digital executions seem to be getting a lot of consumer attention. According to Ibri, this has the team considering a change of media mix to fit the idea rather than vice versa, letting consumers' love define the context while they fall in love with the content. Similarly, "Simple Power" has allowed them to develop some ideas that even transform the packaging itself. In a recent test, General Mills replaced the usual package front with the field of yellow and the single words or simple two-word thoughts, like "Love," "Smile," and "Heart Healthy."

"Simple Power" may be one of Cheerios' most abundant harvests yet.

Virality

05

This chapter features case stories for T-Mobile and Reebok. The common ground for these stories is how they inspired massive social sharing of their messages. By developing videos that captured the popular imagination due to their uniqueness and entertainment value, each brand was able to create a viral bonanza. They reached an astounding number of people without an astounding budget. In both cases, the brands were not leaders in their categories, yet they became as salient as the market leaders.

───────────────────

T-MOBILE CASE STORY

───────────────────

T-Mobile Gets Shared

In April 2011, the British royal family and much of the world were enthralled by the upcoming spectacle of a royal wedding between Prince William Windsor and his bride-to-be Kate Middleton.

Just prior to the big event, a tongue-in-cheek film for T-Mobile appeared on YouTube. It so captured the popular imagination that, according to *Contagious* magazine, it became one of the most shared online advertisements in the world that year.

Despite the fact that the video poked fun at the royal family, Prince William's brother, Prince Harry was so taken with it that he shared it on his personal Facebook page and Twitter account. Rumor has it that he even showed it to his grandmother, the Queen, because he knew she would be amused. So how did T-Mobile create a frenzy of sharing for their online video? It stemmed from their ability to understand what people loved. It was the fruition of three years of inspired content creation that begged to be shared, and which, as a result, helped to sell a lot of mobile phone plans.

T-Mobile's "Dance" was its first big step into capturing emotion and stimulating sharing

Back in 2008, T-Mobile (a division of Deutsche Telekom) focused its marketing strategy on "sharing." This made a lot of sense. The new, more advanced mobile phones offered by the company, supported by their high-speed network, had the speed, connectivity, and high-quality cameras to facilitate sharing, allowing their users to instantly share whatever caught their imagination on the street or online. Sharing was also in tune with the social networking craze that had just started to evolve worldwide. T-Mobile's agency, Saatchi & Saatchi London, captured the strategy first as the thought: "Life is Better When You Share It."

Soon after, it became the pithy advertising line...

"Life's for sharing."

"At first, this line was just a distillation of our client's strategy," explained Richard Huntington, director of strategy at Saatchi London. "It was just a tag line; a good tag line, but little more." Seeing its limitations as a two-dimensional tag line, Huntington, the Saatchi team, and T-Mobile set out to create something three-dimensional, something real that in and of itself could be, wanted to be, and even needed to be shared. They wanted to do rather than just say. In marketing parlance, they wanted to "walk the talk."

Saatchi's executive creative director, Paul Silburn, remembers that the idea needed to do three things: "It had to happen in the real world, not just be an ad. It needed to create something special that people felt compelled to share. Finally, it needed to allow the people watching it to join in." The last point was critical. T-Mobile wanted sharing and participation, which entailed personal engagement to the highest degree possible.

As a strategy on paper it was a great idea. Having the guts to actually execute such an idea, and risk getting it painfully and publicly wrong, was something else entirely. Huntington used the analogy of "people standing by a pool waiting for someone to jump in and tell them how cold the water is" when describing how the key European markets viewed the strategy. In the end, it was the UK that decided to leap.

The team took something novel, interesting, and highly likely to be shared online—the concept of a "flash mob"—and made it something it had never been before—participatory. Flash mobs are groups of people who suddenly assemble in a place for a brief period of time to do something interesting or unusual, before disappearing back into the crowd as quickly as they appeared. In 2008, the most famous flash mob was the Improv Everywhere mob that froze suddenly in New York's Grand Central Station during rush hour, and then unfroze about a minute later. After that, however, flash mobs had been a spectacle to be watched, not something to be a part of. As Silburn put it, "Flash mobs were for showing off. We wanted to create something that was more generous in spirit."

Mass media picked up on the joy and helped spread T-Mobile's message

"Dance" (2009)

T-Mobile chose London's Liverpool Street train station on a cold, dreary January day to work their magic. As commuters walked to their trains, the main waiting room—a giant atrium that can fit thousands of people—came alive to the sound of music (in this case, the Isley Brothers' "Shout"). A few people started dancing, with more and more joining in. Soon the waiting room was full of hundreds of dancers, all in highly synchronized movement. But they did not look like professional dancers. They were dressed just like everyday commuters: some in jeans, some in suits and ties. The music changed to a waltz to disco to rock and more. Each time the music changed, the dancers were joined by yet more dancers. Their movements were beautifully choreographed. There were 400 dancers in all (chosen from 10,000 auditions). The performance lasted about three minutes. During the dance, commuters did just what T-Mobile and Saatchi hoped they would. They took out their phones and shared what they had seen with calls, texts, photos, and videos to family and friends. Better still, many joined in and celebrated the morning rush hour by dancing along with smiles and laughter.

What happened next exceeded the wildest expectations of Saatchi or T-Mobile. Television news and tabloid press were awash with stories of the unique event. News shows featured videos of the event, combining footage provided by T-Mobile (gathered from 10 hidden cameras) with user-generated footage from the public. *The Sun* newspaper reflected the general opinion of all the press corps by saying that T-Mobile's "Dance" created an "Epidemic of Joy" in the heart of central London. The timing was perfect. The country was gripped by recession. People were in the post-Christmas blues, dampened by London's dark winter skies. This was a breath of much-needed fresh air, whether you were there in person or watching it somewhere else.

"It took a lot of trust and it redefined the way we worked at Saatchi."

Within 36 hours of the event, Saatchi and the T-Mobile marketing team had edited video and photographs, turning it into a fully integrated advertising campaign, both online and on-air. The centerpiece of the campaign was a three-minute film that ran on television as a roadblock (i.e., running at the exact same time on all major stations). At this point T-Mobile had a big decision to make. How product-based should the commercial be? They went back and forth. In the end, they decided to let the joy of the moment and the overall idea speak for itself, with the spot simply showing the event as it happened. The film finished with just the T-Mobile logo and their endline "Life's for Sharing," while showing people at the event sharing with their friends via their phones.

Downplaying the commercialism was a key decision. The team's experience was that when a message was more like an advertisement, it was less likely to be viewed. When it was less like an advertisement, it was more likely to be viewed. Regardless of the lack of explicit commercialism, consumers picked up on the message and gave T-Mobile credit for bringing them the idea with a minimum of hard sell. Importantly, research showed that consumers played back all kinds of positive product attributes for the brand as a result of the ad, in large part because they loved the brand for what it had done, not because the ad explicitly stated the attributes. This learning is a cornerstone of Lovemarks thinking: engage the emotions and the brain follows.

Kelly Engstrom is the senior advertising manager at T-Mobile. She described "Dance" as "a new, brave and sometimes very scary experience." There were none of the trappings usually associated with presenting an advertising idea to senior management. There were no storyboards or scripts for example. "It took a lot of trust, and it redefined the way we worked with Saatchi. We worked together at every step. We were all in the editing room together at 3 a.m. It forged a very tight team."

"Dance" "Sing-along"

"Dance" was a monumental creative and commercial success. By 2010, it had climbed to the top 10 in viewership for all viral videos. In addition, over 95,000 people downloaded the film via Bluetooth-enabled outdoor digital screens, making it the most popular Transvision Bluetooth campaign to date. It generated over £8 million in free publicity. For a brand that was not the market leader, not even number two, and which was being outspent by significantly bigger competitors, the idea was a home run.

The event enabled people to discover and become part of "Life's for Sharing," through personal experience, offline media, and online or social media, creating a physical manifestation of T-Mobile's beliefs and capabilities. And if sharing was the key marketing goal, then it was grandly achieved. In addition to the 35 million views on YouTube to date, the event has inspired 68 different Facebook groups. From a business perspective, "Dance" was measured to have delivered £15 million of incremental sales.

"Sing-along" was a follow-up to "Dance"

Engstrom believes the greatest achievement of "Dance" was to give the brand salience: "We believed we had something special, but we did not anticipate how quickly this would put T-Mobile on the map with consumers. It put us firmly in their minds, almost overnight, and allowed us to have a conversation with them about our products."

"Sing-along" (2009)

At first thought, following up an idea like "Dance" seemed pretty daunting. But in this case it was not. The public had become enthralled with "Dance," so much so that fan-based Facebook groups even staged re-enactments of the dance in supermarkets and shopping centers. A common theme of online discussion was that people wished they had been lucky enough to be there in person when it had originally happened. With that kind of pent-up demand, T-Mobile and Saatchi aimed to create another event that was an even bigger, bolder expression of sharing. This time, however, they would leak information to stir the pent-up interest, and they would have the idea work as a single pan-European campaign to drive a consistent brand message across multiple markets.

The new idea had to have all three of the key criteria that Paul Silburn had outlined earlier. This time, however, instead of dancing, the creative team thought:

"What if the brand did some singing?"

Thus, in 2009, "Sing-along" was born.

. . . .

The idea was on an even bigger scale than "Dance." T-Mobile would throw a mass-participation public party in London's iconic Trafalgar Square, where anyone could come along and join in singing karaoke.

To build anticipation, they posted on Facebook fan groups that something would be happening in Trafalgar Square at 6 p.m. on April 30, 2009. They also sent "pass it on" SMS messages to London T-Mobile customers and sparked rumors via "leaks" to London radio stations. Buzz about the event became so big that the Metropolitan Police had to ask T-Mobile to stop talking about it because they were afraid the gigantic square would be mobbed. In the end, over 13,500 people turned up. More than 8,000 microphones were passed out for people to sing along for an hour to some of their favorite songs on a huge projected screen, karaoke-style.

The first song was the Beatles' "Hey Jude." Its infectious chorus of "Nah, Nah, Nahs" instantly got the crowd going. People shared microphones with strangers, put their arms around each other, singing, smiling, and laughing. The crowd then got stuck into Janice Joplin's "Take Another Little Piece of My Heart," another belt-it-out tune. Halfway through the song, something unexpected happened. A young woman in blue jeans and hooded coat jumped up on a makeshift stage and was shown on the monitors. When she pulled her hood back, it was international singing star P!nk, making the event instantly more memorable and giving people more reason than ever to share what was happening.

Twenty-seven film cameras and several photographers worked across the event, capturing footage and images for market-specific communications. Aside from P!nk, who was known in all European markets, other markets seeded the crowd with local singing stars of their own. For example, Nina Badric of Croatia was in the crowd. She is immensely popular not just in Croatia, but Bosnia and Herzegovia, Montenegro, Slovenia, and Turkey. Not everyone would know who she was at the time, but when the video of the event was later turned into local marketing material, her appearance, and the appearance of other local celebrities, would make the campaign special and shareable in markets throughout Europe.

As with "Dance," "Sing-along" presented a huge production challenge for the agency team. Every one of the advertising elements—video, audio, and print—for a three-month campaign needed to be captured in just one hour. By comparison, a simple 30-second television commercial shoot can last for two 14-hour production days. Saatchi's Huntington remembers that the whole day was "just crazy," but also remembers being in the middle of the crowd and realizing that "it was a moment I would never, ever forget."

Anticipation left over from the first event had become fuel for the next event. Although "Sing-along" never matched "Dance" for total online views, it still broke the massive 10 million-view barrier. It also led to more user-generated content being posted on the Web. In the end, it got more press coverage than "Dance," delivering more value in free media. It was less viewed, but actually more famous.

Over 13,500 people gathered in Trafalgar Square

"Royal Wedding" (2011)

Between 2009 and 2011 T-Mobile extended the "Life's for Sharing" campaign with a number of other sharable ideas. In late 2009, they introduced "Josh's Band." In support of T-Mobile's unlimited text and internet deal, they asked consumers,

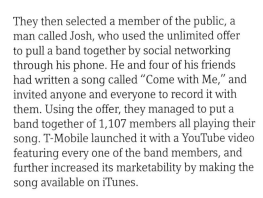

"What would you do if you had unlimited text and internet?"

....

They then selected a member of the public, a man called Josh, who used the unlimited offer to pull a band together by social networking through his phone. He and four of his friends had written a song called "Come with Me," and invited anyone and everyone to record it with them. Using the offer, they managed to put a band together of 1,107 members all playing their song. T-Mobile launched it with a YouTube video featuring every one of the band members, and further increased its marketability by making the song available on iTunes.

In 2010, T-Mobile was singing again. This time they greeted unsuspecting passengers at London's Heathrow Airport International Terminal with a crowd of 300 people who spontaneously burst into synchronized song, giving weary travelers a welcome home they would never forget. The uniquely talented ensemble consisted not only of traditional singers, but of a "vocal orchestra"—vocalists using their voices to recreate sounds of instruments, including guitars, violins, cellos, flutes, and drums. Some of the numbers were soft and romantic, others fun and raucous.

For the brand, these campaigns were very successful. They built on the "Life's for Sharing" equity and supported T-Mobile's product offerings, delivering on their marketing goals. In fact, "Welcome Back" was the second-most-awarded piece of advertising in the world in 2011, according to the Gunn Report. Despite this, the team knew there must be another really huge idea out there, one that would get the kind of resonance they had seen from "Dance" and "Sing-along."

This time, the idea was not based on a brief. It was not planned. The Saatchi team developed it as a speculative idea based on the coincidence of two things. The first thing was the once-in-an-epoch marriage of a royal prince with a direct line to the throne—along with the associated hullabaloo—planned for April 29, 2011. It was going to be a worldwide cultural phenomenon. The other thing was the popularity on YouTube of surprise wedding marches that turned traditional walks down the aisle into all-out production numbers, dances and/or rap performances. YouTube had dozens of such videos and many were wildly popular.

The agency's creative team decided to create an "alternative" royal wedding—the one the British public wished would happen—using royal look-alikes and launching it online two weeks before the real wedding took place. The staid royal family was about to rap and boogie their way down the aisle of Westminster Abbey.

By this time T-Mobile was used to taking risks. As Richard Huntington pointed out,

"There is no such thing as a good or bad client, just clients who have confidence and those who lack it..."

"...T-Mobile had confidence and so did we. We had built a new type of client-agency relationship. They were there with us every step of the way. There was mutual trust that we both wanted to do something great."

This idea would be really risky however. It would be making fun of the royal family. If they got it right, they would have one of their biggest hits. If they got it wrong, well, perhaps it was not too good to even contemplate that.

The team pulled together royal look-alikes from all over England. By the time they were done, they had assembled a troupe that looked exactly like the royal wedding party. They were all there: the Queen, Prince Philip, Prince Charles, Camilla, Princess Anne, William, Harry, Kate Middleton, and even the Archbishop of Canterbury. When the doors to the cathedral opened, the party came down the aisle, not to *Pomp and Circumstance* or Pachelbel's *Canon*, but to the hard-rocking tune "House of Love" by the British boy band East 17. Every member of the royal family was dancing in exaggerated and slightly inappropriate ways. Even watching it today, over a year later, there is only one word that truly captures it: hilarious!

T-Mobile and Saatchi were counting on the public, and especially the young royals, to see the humor as tongue-in-cheek and to have a big laugh. They did. As we have mentioned, Prince Harry even put it on his Facebook page saying that it was "…a taste of what you will see at Westminster Abbey."

The film was, of course, meant to be shared. It sparked thousands of conversations on YouTube, Twitter, and Facebook, including many Americans who were confused as to whether it was the real royal wedding or not. It was the second-most-viewed video of 2011, after Volkswagen's charming "Darth Vader" commercial. With the addition of "Royal Wedding," T-Mobile's "Life's for Sharing" videos have now garnered over 100 million views! In terms of return on investment, T-Mobile estimates that "Royal Wedding" provided £6 in economic return for every £1 spent on it.

Market results for the campaign have been outstanding. "Dance" and "Royal Wedding" alone have been measured to increase sales, share, brand consideration, retail footfall (store traffic), sales conversion, and average revenue per user, and to lower cost of acquisition and product churn.

Lysa Hardy, who was head of brand and communications at T-Mobile UK at the time of the "Dance" launch, said of the new campaign:

"This new media strategy represented a brave move for us and was a resounding success. Not only did we capture the imagination of the nation but we also delivered for the business."

....

The Institute for Practitioners in Advertising (IPA), which gave the campaign a silver award in 2010, put the business-building power of the idea into proper context in their Editor's Summary:

"During the worst recession since the 1930s, T-Mobile faced diminishing returns in a contracting market; mobile phone usage was cut by a third, and T-Mobile was an unloved brand. Running counter to the prevailing actions of the cut-price offers from competitors, T-Mobile used the recession to revitalize the brand and win over new high-value contract customers. The 'Life's for Sharing' campaign was created to give people something they valued, to celebrate and share with their loved ones."

In their 2012 book *Spending Advertising Money in a Digital Age: How to Navigate the Media Flow*, Hamish Pringle and Jim Marshall credit T-Mobile with elevating outdoor media to a level where Marshall McLuhan would have been proud: "The T-Mobile campaign based around the concept of filmed live events, such as the one at London's Liverpool Street station, is clearly an idea where medium and message are inextricably linked."

By perfectly meshing medium, audience, and message, T-Mobile has consistently given Britain, and much of Europe, what they love. Kelly Engstrom noted that, at the start, T-Mobile was not loved or even well known. She said, "To become a Lovemark, we needed to do something great for the consumer."

Engstrom often presents the T-Mobile case study to university students. Her advice for them when trying to create a Lovemark is "be brave." "If you aren't brave enough to do something refreshing and new, it doesn't matter how big your budget is. You will not get people to care because you don't care enough to do something fresh. To achieve success, T-Mobile and the agency needed to innovate for the consumer. We had to go out on a limb!"

──────────

──────────

Reebok Reinvents a Classic

On the other side of the world, another company was hoping to leverage a YouTube video to viral success, just as T-Mobile had done. Reebok and Saatchi & Saatchi Fallon in Japan started this quest with an innovative product and a list of marketing limitations.

The innovative product was Reebok's "Taikan" line of athletic clothing. Unlike other athletic clothing, the Taikan line had a functional benefit beyond being light or comfortable or wicking away your sweat (all of which it did). It actually fitted to your body in such a way as to improve your posture. Optimal posture encourages optimal breathing, core flexibility, balance, and strength, all of which can lead to improved athletic performance.

What agency wouldn't want to advertise such a product?

The marketing limitations were daunting however. The product was aimed at a mass market of anyone, man or woman, who engaged in any manner of sports activity. Unfortunately, Reebok was a late entrant into the sports-performance clothing segment, and it was being vastly outspent by competitors such as Nike, Under Armour, and Adidas. Add to this the fact that the idea of clothing leading to better posture, leading to enhanced performance, needed a lot of explaining.

Phillip Rubel, CEO of Saatchi & Saatchi Fallon in Tokyo, explained, "Given our budget and everything we had to communicate, our strategy rested on creating something so good and interesting that it would go viral." It would have to become popular online and cross over into mainstream news media in order to get the results Reebok wanted. But in the end, very few things actually go viral. The internet is littered with marketers' "viral" videos that never were.

What made Reebok's attempt different, and successful, was that they uncovered big insights that helped lead to a breakthrough idea. According to Rubel,

"We got great insights because Lovemarks thinking permeated the process, from the way we built the strategy to the research we conducted to the brainstorming we did. When you know what you are looking for, it is easier to find."

....

The first big insight was that the average sports hobbyist, regardless of age or gender, was looking for the advantage that a new piece of equipment would give them. Their closets were littered with the new tennis racquets, golf clubs and/or ski equipment that they thought at the time would improve their game. Reebok and Saatchi Fallon imagined an alternative to that cycle: Taikan would help you improve your core instead of your equipment. A better you, rather than you with better equipment, had the potential to be a wake-up call to the market.

The second insight provided the key to reaching the broad audience Reebok needed. Nearly everyone in Japan, regardless of age or gender, is familiar with Japanese TV network NHK's morning exercise show entitled *Rajio Taiso* and connects it to ideal physical conditioning. The show was a popular and historical icon in Japan, whether people watched it or not. "Rajio taiso" means "radio conditioning," as the show was originally named when it was broadcast on the radio in the 1920s, before it became a TV show.

Rajio Taiso was a low-budget production that consisted of nothing more than a stage on which three individuals clad in gym clothes performed calisthenics (the one in the middle was usually seated to represent the elderly or handicapped), accompanied by an off-camera piano to help keep the pace and an announcer's voice calling out the routines.

The exercises were designed so that almost anyone of any age could follow along while watching the show. In fact, *Rajio Taiso* was so popular that schools, factory workers, office workers, firemen, store staff, and just about anyone who watched TV would do it together to build a sense of unity. It was a common sight to see groups of people performing the *Rajio Taiso* routine together at the start of their work or school day. In a group-oriented society like Japan, such daily group activities are well accepted. Over the years, *Rajio Taiso* had renewed itself in three successful television iterations (*Rajio Taiso 1*, *2*, and *3*), each pretty much the same as its predecessor.

Reebok Taikan
reinvents a classic:
"Rajio Taiso 4"

Introducing Rajio Taiso 4

The agency proposed for Reebok to hijack the *Rajio Taiso* phenomenon and launch their own new version: *Rajio Taiso 4*. Instead of the three people clad in gym clothes, they enlisted three gymnastic contortionists, clad in Reebok Taikan clothing, who started out doing the normal expected routines, but soon surprised viewers by performing near-impossible acts of balance, flexibility, and strength. To keep the viewers guessing and blur the lines of reality, there was no branding whatsoever until the very end of the performance, when the camera zoomed in on the Taikan logo on the leg of one of the performers. A website address was listed underneath the video which was posted on YouTube.

To seed the campaign, flyers were distributed at several train station exits in downtown Tokyo and Osaka announcing that the "4th Generation of *Rajio Taiso*" had arrived. The video was sent to the PR departments of major web portals in the hope they would feature the video. But other than that, it was all up to the video on YouTube to go viral. Fingers were firmly crossed.

Results Beyond the Wildest Dreams

The Reebok team set some realistic objectives for this campaign. They hoped to get 10,000 views in the first day and 100,000 by the end of the first month. Based on their budget of 11 million yen (about US $140,000) that would have equated to a modest success. Instead they got 135,000 views the first day. In their first month they surpassed one million views. By the end of the campaign, they had over 2.3 million views.

In addition, the campaign ended up getting 550 million yen (US $7 million) of free exposure as virtually every television station picked up the video and showed a clip, some shows even going so far as to invite the performers and the Reebok marketing team to appear live. NHK did a feature on the Reebok film.

Further still, people began to try to imitate the performers' moves, and posted their own videos. Football teams, cheerleaders, badminton teams, and various others did their best to copy the routines of the contortionists. Only one aspiring ballerina truly came close.

Dieter Haberl, head of Reebok in Japan, felt the campaign was not only successful, but fit perfectly into the Japanese cultural landscape. He said, "*Rajio Taiso* was an excellent example of how Reebok was able to tap into the cultural relevancy of our target audience here in Japan. In fact, the underlying principle of the 'construction' of the clothing technology is derived from the Japanese approach to fitness, with posture and breathing firmly at its center."

In the end, Reebok's "Rajio Taiso 4" was the second-most-viewed online video in Japan in 2010 (surpassed only by a famous Japanese fashion model's steamy online shoot). It used Lovemarks thinking to tap into the collective memory of the audience and reinvent, in a positive way, something the audience had always felt strongly about.

What made it a great Lovemarks idea was that the reinvention created the perfect platform to show off the product's competitive points of difference.

Rallying Cries

06

This chapter features case stories for Lenovo and Lexus. The common ground for these stories is how they created advertising ideas that became rallying cries, not just for their customers but also for their employees. These rallying cries gave the people who worked on the brands a sense of purpose that helped direct everything they did, from product development to customer service to marketing and beyond. These stories compare brand experiences that are decades apart, but which teach the same lesson, whether 20 years ago, today, or tomorrow.

LENOVO CASE STORY

Lenovo: Starting the Journey

One of the most interesting reality programs in Mexico won't be found on TV. It is on the web. The program is called *Los Doers*. Produced in partnership with MTV Mexico, the show features four young Latin Americans who have been chosen for their unique practical abilities. They are:

Sebastian, *a Mexican industrial designer capable of building anything with any material.*

Mox, *a Peruvian social networker with literally millions of friends in his network.*

Ann-Marie, *a Colombian trend finder or "cool hunter," who finds out what people will want next.*

Nico, *an Argentinean computer programmer, who can solve the most difficult computer-based problems.*

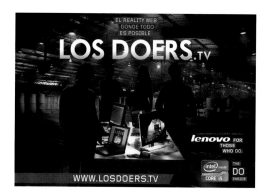

In Mexico, "Los Doers" solve seemingly impossible tasks using Lenovo's latest computers

During each eight-minute episode the "Doers" are given a seemingly impossible task to solve in 72 hours using their combined skills.

The ideas for the tasks are contributed online by ordinary people. In one episode the team needed to help a disabled person start surfing. In another, they had to build a car using only things they could get in a supermarket. In yet another, they needed to find a way to get the world's most famous soccer player, FC Barcelona's Lionel Messi, on a Skype call with them.

The team does have a secret weapon however. They have been equipped with the latest generation of Lenovo's most capable computers.

Lenovo Who?

To Americans, for example, Lenovo is still a little-known brand name. The company got its start when its founder, Liu Chuanzhi—known to employees as "Chairman Liu"— was assigned to work for the Chinese Academy of Sciences, fresh from the turmoil of the Cultural Revolution. In 1984, with about $25,000 worth of funding from the academy, he started the company that is now Lenovo, in the Chinese equivalent of Dave Packard's garage—a guard shack on the outskirts of Beijing.

By 1997, Lenovo was China's number one PC maker. But its biggest move came in 2005 when it bought IBM's PC business and the well-known "ThinkPad" brand for just under $2 billion. The purchase made Liu something of a national hero; but it also led to years of struggle in order to manage what *Fast Company* magazine called a "corporate marriage of immense complexity." That struggle would forge today's Lenovo, which has emerged as a complex, well-managed, multinational company with an ethnically diverse management team based in cities all over the world.

Today's Lenovo is an incomparable combination of the strengths of East and West. It has over 26,000 global employees, and it is redefining what we think we know about Chinese brands. In 2011 and 2012, for example, Lenovo was ranked number one in the Computer Reliability Report. The latest report put it three places ahead of Apple and five places ahead of Hewlett-Packard.

Lenovo's Challenge

Lenovo's challenge is to create a global brand that reflects the high performance and quality of their products and manufacturing capability. So, in early 2011 they held an advertising agency pitch to get ideas on how to build a consistent brand globally, despite the fact that their existing awareness and image varied significantly from country to country. Outside of China—where Lenovo had dominant market share and wide awareness—key countries where the brand would need to succeed were Mexico, US, Japan, India, Russia, and Brazil. Ultimately, the winning advertising campaign would run in over 32 countries.

How different were these key countries for Lenovo? In America, the brand had extremely low awareness, but their ThinkPad product still had equity. In Mexico, Lenovo had a significant growth opportunity, but was being outspent by its competitors 3-to-1. In Japan, which is a mature and very sophisticated computer market, Lenovo had to overcome the common perception that Chinese products are low quality. In India, Lenovo was already number two with 10% market share, in a market where nearly 50% of the population is under 25 years old.

Finding a single global idea—an idea that would be as relevant for building the fledgling brand in America as for the powerful brand in India, and everywhere in between—was Lenovo's great hope. David Roman, the company's senior vice president and chief marketing officer, was a man with an unswerving focus on this result. His previous 14 years at Apple and five years at Hewlett-Packard in top advertising and marketing posts had made him a believer in the power of big, consistent, global ideas.

Being Good Versus Being Pretty

The agency pitch process was pretty standard. It started with eight agencies presenting their credentials to Lenovo management. The agencies paid a visit to Lenovo's US headquarters in Raleigh, North Carolina. Ultimately, four selected agencies would pitch for the global campaign, one of them being Saatchi & Saatchi New York.

The Saatchi team did what any good agency would do. They immersed themselves in the product and the product's consumer. Following their trip to Raleigh, they were left with a tremendous impression of how focused the company and its employees were on creating the best products in the market with a peak performance culture to match.

The products impressed them. Admittedly, they were not the prettiest personal computers. They did not have the design appeal of Apple, for example. But the products could do amazing things. They would start immediately, no waiting for things to load. They were made with spill-resistant keyboards. Drop your soda straight onto your PC? Not a problem. Just wipe it up and keep going. And as we have seen from the Computer Reliability Report, these machines could be counted on for a long time.

One product story that really inspired the Saatchi team was a letter from a woman who had literally just put the finishing touches on her PhD dissertation on her Lenovo, only to get into a huge car accident on her way to turn it in. The car was totaled, the computer beat up badly, but the Lenovo still worked and the dissertation was safe and sound.

One thing the Saatchi team couldn't help but notice when they visited Raleigh was Lenovo's mantra, which was prominently displayed throughout the facility: "We Do What We Say and Own What We Do."

This collection of short words went to the core of what Lenovo was all about. In other words, don't just say it, do it! This was a company that was not about fluff, and it was a company that stood behind its decisions and its products.

The target audience for the new campaign had been identified as Millennials—teens and twenty-somethings—worldwide. According to Roman,

"I don't believe you can have a technology brand that doesn't come from the youth market today."

To get an understanding of these potential consumers and their relationship with technology, the pitch team combed through mountains of research available from syndicated sources such as Yankelovich and Mintel. To get deeper insights, Saatchi New York sent their planners on Xploring visits to all the key markets, and tapped into other planners from Saatchi offices throughout the world for insights into secondary markets.

According to Jane Wagner, executive vice president at Saatchi New York, who helped run the pitch, the big idea came out of a confluence of what the client stood for and what Millennials valued. One consistent message that came from the Xploring trips was that Millennials cared less about how pretty their computer looked and a lot more about what it could do. They wanted to achieve, but on their own terms. As often happens, one consumer became the epitome of what many in the target audience were saying. In the case of the Lenovo pitch, that person was a young DJ from a Tokyo nightclub who was using five Lenovo's to mix his musical magic. He became the team's poster child.

Lenovo user Raymond Li designed and built from scratch a water-propelled jetpack, something everyone said couldn't be built

He told them:

"Computers are not a badge; they are a tool."

This consumer truth jibed with the stories that Lenovo had told the agency team about how consumers did the coolest things with their products—be they farmers in China running the entire farm operation on a Lenovo, or people in America chasing hurricanes with their durable, trusty Lenovos at their side.

When the team put all of this together with the company's mantra, the idea jumped to life:

Lenovo, For Those Who Do.

....

The emphasis is on doing versus being pretty. As people at Lenovo like to say, "If Apple's style is style, then substance is our style." Claudine Cheever, chief strategy officer at Saatchi New York, explained it this way: "When we looked at all of the competitive advertising worldwide, it fell into three categories. There was Apple. There were those who were trying to be like Apple. And there were those who were apologizing for not being Apple." This idea was different. It hit on a consumer truth and a product truth. It positioned Lenovo as the "Anti-Mac." It had the opportunity to differentiate Lenovo from Apple, and from everyone else.

Interestingly enough, the team came up with the idea that the computers were for "doing" long before they developed the final line. The working line was "We are those that do." In a twist of the usual joke where the agency CEO claims to have thought up the successful campaign line, this final version of the line was actually blurted out by Saatchi & Saatchi New York CEO Mary Baglivo in a team meeting. It wasn't a big change, but the focus on "For Those Who Do" gave it the necessary edge and focus.

Mary calls Lenovo a "crazy, fun pitch." The pitch took place in Las Vegas in the middle of the technology industry's biggest global event: the Consumer Electronics Show (CES). Belying the high tech surroundings, the team entered the pitch room to find it was freezing cold with no sound system and no internet access. After sorting out the technology, things warmed up decidedly when the agency ran the video showcasing their idea. "For Those Who Do" resonated with Lenovo immediately.

Alan Hallberg is vice president of global brand communication at Lenovo. He noted that the line has become a rallying cry: "The line strikes a chord internally. Employees really see that it is an accurate representation of how they look at the company, whether it is in China or in the US." He believes that when a communication line becomes more than an advertising slogan you get "outsized benefits," because every one of your employees becomes a brand ambassador for the campaign. One example of how the campaign was internalized by rank and file employees was when, unbeknownst to the marketing group, Lenovo's sales and service group started calling themselves "The Do Crew."

A Global Idea

The Saatchi team knew they were onto a global idea even before the client's reaction. When they shared the idea with planners from Saatchi offices in other countries during the pitch process, they were told that the idea worked, and that each country could find relevant ways to execute it for their consumers. The idea tapped into a global truth about the target audience that none of the competitors recognized. Interestingly enough, their biggest challenge came in the home country of China, where the word "do" implied blind obedience, like one lemming following another. But when the Chinese character for "do" was combined with the character for "think," which gave it the meaning of "smart do" as opposed to "passive do," the idea worked there too.

DJs use Lenovo's
"Do Machines" to
mix musical magic

In order to make sure the idea was developed correctly for each market, the planners in each Saatchi office created "word clouds" that captured each country's unique consumer.

INDIA

DOING IT FOR REAL

move on without moving away
integrity authenticity perseverance energy
intensity duality satisfy can't help myself release
alter ego testing boundaries mad heart free falling rough and ready
fantasy meets reality adventure delirious
walking the walk obsession burning desire
testing limits labor of love passion

JAPAN

DO IT SIMPLE-ZOKU

tech savvy pragmatic authentic integrity slowing down
humble respectful empowered back to basics contradicting agile
genuine integrity empowered streamlining fluid open
many passions confident analog

The campaign burst onto the worldwide scene in April 2011. In the US, for example, a 60-second launch TV commercial told the uninitiated American consumer:

The world won't move forward by itself.

It needs a push, a shove, a hard shoulder to the ribs. And it needs people with the drive and imagination to do it. People who refuse to sit around and wait for the next great evolution.

The people who do.

The ones who tinker, who build, who create.

And we make the machines that help them.

Do machines.

Superpowered creation engines perfectly optimized to help the people who do...do more... do better...do what's never been done. We're not just about what we make. We're for the inspired thinkers who roll up their sleeves and make things happen...

Lenovo.
For those who do.

A US print ad based on how
Millennials use their PCs as
tools rather than ornaments

The campaign rolled out with television commercials, sponsorships, print ads, outdoor, digital ads, in-store displays, online games, and even augmented reality displays from Tokyo to Frankfurt to Moscow to Delhi and beyond. In each case, the materials were tied to the big global idea, but also designed specifically for the unique qualities of that market's consumers. Many ads featured the specific stories told by consumers during the Xploring phase.

The idea was simple and powerful enough that different agencies in different countries were able to execute and coordinate seamlessly. For example, the *Los Doers* reality program in Mexico was developed by a local Mexican agency, named AC. The show had 1.3 million uploads in just two months.

The Results

In markets where Lenovo was not well known, like the United States, an obvious goal was to drive awareness. In all markets, the ultimate goal was to drive consideration for the brand, which is the metric that ultimately drives more sales.

From July 2011 to January 2012 unaided consideration among consumers 18–34 years old increased in the United States from 11.1% to 17.3%. In Japan, it increased from 8.2% to 12.3%. In Mexico, it increased from 20.8% to 25.3%. Increases were seen in every key market. Increases were also seen across the board for the core 18–24 age group, which Lenovo calls the "Net Generation."

The campaign has been part of a global marketing, merchandising, and distribution push that has already seen Lenovo move from the fourth-largest to the second-largest computer manufacturer in the world in just the last 18 months.

In the just-reported third quarter 2012 results, Lenovo edged past HP in total shipments to claim the number one position. That Lenovo will become the number one PC maker for all of 2012, when fourth quarter results are tabulated in a few months, is a definite possibility. That would mean that Lenovo became number one four years ahead of its goal.

Lovemark or not a Lovemark?

The Lenovo campaign is just over a year old. In markets like China, Lenovo is already a Lovemark and a national symbol of pride. In India, it is already one of the most respected brands. In markets like the US, Mexico, Russia, Japan, and Germany the brand still has a long way to go. It is striking to think of a brand that is already number two worldwide as being an outlier brand in much of the rest of the world with lots of room for growth versus the competition. But that's what it is.

Will it become a global Lovemark? We'll see. But one thing is for sure, the core idea, "For Those Who Do," is true to the emotions of Millennials worldwide. It also reflects the ethos of a company that has a democratic view of innovation, and which builds some of the best computers on earth.

In 1998, more than a decade before winning the Lenovo business, Saatchi & Saatchi CEO Worldwide Kevin Roberts told an audience in Shanghai that one of the company's key goals was

"to be involved in the first Chinese brand to go global."

If early results are anything to go by, Lenovo is well on its way.

LEXUS CASE STORY

Lexus Pursues Perfection

Lenovo's campaign line, "For Those Who Do," captured the ethos of the company for its employees and consumers alike. A similar story occurred for Saatchi's Team One agency in California and their key client, Lexus.

When Lexus was launched in the US in 1989, the idea of a Japanese luxury car was an oxymoron. Japanese cars were famous for being small, reliable, and great on gas. They had never put out a car that could compete with Mercedes, BMW, or Cadillac.

In order to position the car, Team One knew that Lexus had to stand for something different. The world did not need a copycat luxury car. The agency's first step was to visit Japan. They talked directly to the engineers who designed the car, including the car's chief engineer, Ichiro Suzuki. They visited the factories where the car was being built.

Just as the Saatchi New York team was inspired by Lenovo's mission, Team One was inspired by the Lexus philosophy. In the early 1980s, Toyota Motor Corporation's chairman, Eiji Toyoda, challenged the company to make "the finest luxury car ever built." In order to do this, the engineering team took the best luxury cars in the world and disassembled them, looking at every individual piece. Their strategy was to apply the company's ethos of *kaizen* or "continuous improvement" not just to the vehicle as a whole, but to every part. They would build the finest luxury car ever built, improved piece by improved piece.

As a result, the first Lexus LS 400 was awarded over 300 patents. By contrast, if a typical new car has one or two new patents it is usually cause for celebration. At first, the agency became enamored of the sheer number of innovations. They considered advertising lines such as "It's More than a Car, It's an Invention." In the end, however, they realized that the story was not just about this one car, but an almost maniacal dedication to a philosophy of making every luxury car better than the last—kaizen.

Inventive demonstrations, like the one in this television commercial from the early 1990s, helped give Lexus a strong reputation for pursuing perfection with consumers

Kaizen became "The Relentless Pursuit of Perfection." It captured the uniqueness of the product completely. This was the best-built luxury car in the market. Importantly, for the newly formed Lexus division at Toyota Motor Sales USA, it too became a rallying cry. It summarized in simple English words what their division was all about. They had been working for years before the car's launch to pursue perfection by creating new dealership, sales, marketing, and service experiences to match the quality of the automobile. Now they had a phrase that made it clear to everyone who worked there—and to the loads of new employees they would be hiring—what their mission was.

Scott Gilbert was the management director running the launch for Team One. He remembers: "A number of things came together to give everyone at Lexus a feeling that 'The Relentless Pursuit of Perfection' was more than a tag line. This thought was really an announcement that Lexus could and would go above and beyond in everything it did." For example, in its first year, Lexus was number one in the industry in initial quality. That was astounding: the first year of production is when any car usually has its most defects. The way Lexus handled any small defects that did occur was astounding too, including, according to Gilbert, flying a service team up to Montana to fix a minor problem on actor Harrison Ford's new car.

The "Relentless Pursuit of Perfection" was also a perfect reflection of the "Lexus Covenant," a pledge that all Lexus employees still sign when they join the brand. It states unequivocally that Lexus will make "the finest cars ever built…will have the finest dealer network…[and] will treat each customer as we would a guest in our own home."

The campaign theme and the Covenant continue to exhilarate the people who work at Lexus, over 20 years later. According to Mark Templin, the current general manager of the Lexus Division, "Since our brand's inception in 1989, the Lexus Covenant has guided our every business decision. Our consistent adherence to one of its main tenets—to treat each customer like we would a guest in our own home—changed the luxury automobile industry forever. Twenty-three years later, the 'Pursuit of Perfection' continues to inspire us and our dealer partners to do better every day."

Consumers have responded by consistently making Lexus one of the best-selling luxury nameplates in the United States.

♥

More Than a Brand

This chapter features case stories for Safeguard soap and The Ritz-Carlton. The common ground for these stories is that they understood that the product they offered had the potential to be much more than a product, or even a brand. Luxury hotels are a home away from home for business travelers, and a place where vacationers go to experience something special. Soap in developing countries is far more than a way to get your hands clean. It can actually improve the life of your family. The teams running these widely disparate brands thought big and did not underestimate the brands' emotional impact on their consumers. By doing so, they ran past their competition and became more than brands.

SAFEGUARD CASE STORY

Safeguard Gets in Tune with Chinese Moms

The year is about 470 BCE. The great Chinese philosopher Confucius is conversing with his student and disciple Zengzi. He is expounding on the concept of "Xiao" or filial piety.

In essence, he tells his student that the highest virtue for individuals and society is to show obedience and respect for their parents and ancestors. Confucius and Zengzi's conversations are enshrined in *Xiao Jing*, "The Classic of Xiao," one of the most important texts in Chinese history.

Confucius' thoughts on family loyalty and respect, formed over 2000 years ago, have had an enormous influence on Chinese culture and history. Admittedly, China has experienced tumultuous changes in the 20th century with warlordism, Japanese invasion, civil war, and the advent of Communism. Cultural change has been especially pronounced in the last 30 years since Deng Xiaoping reputedly first uttered the phrase, "To get rich is glorious"—a phrase he may not have actually said, but which nonetheless helped ignite entrepreneurial forces held dormant in a dynamic, entrepreneurial culture. Notwithstanding these recent economic and social changes, filial piety remains at the core of what it means to be Chinese.

Historically, this heightened sense of family loyalty led to large families and even larger extended families, or clans, living together under one roof or compound. In 1979, however, in order to fight China's population explosion, the government introduced the Family Planning Policy, also known as the "One-Child Policy." It stipulates that married urban couples may only have one child, while allowing some specific exemptions. It applies to almost 40% of China's families.

While this policy has always been controversial, and may sound draconian, China's population now stands at over 1.3 billion people or 20% of the world's population, four times the population of the world's third most populous country (the United States), on a land mass that is slightly smaller. Urban overcrowding has become a big problem. Shanghai now has over 23 million inhabitants, and China has over 150 cities of one million people or more. By comparison, the United States has only nine cities with over one million people.

Chinese parents are to a degree obsessed with the future of their children.

....

Modern China has a tension between its culture, which values strong, extended family relationships, and the requirement to have only one child. Understanding that tension and helping to resolve it for Chinese moms is at the heart of how Safeguard soap created a Lovemark in China.

Focus on the Child

The Lovemarks journey for Safeguard in China actually started in the Philippines. Safeguard had been popular in both countries for years, selling soap by focusing on the product's superior functional qualities of anti-bacterial germ protection. The Philippines then successfully focused on where germ protection mattered most: helping moms protect their families against everyday health problems.

This was important emotional territory in a developing country, where exposure to the germs that cause maladies like colds, flu, and diarrhea, and exposure to parasites such as roundworm, are all too common. How important is anti-bacterial soap and hand washing in this scenario? Medical research indicates that 80% of infectious diseases are carried by germs that are picked up and passed on by hand.

In the early 2000s, the team at Procter & Gamble (the makers of Safeguard) and Saatchi & Saatchi decided to apply this strategy to China as well. In China, however, the campaign would focus on the health of a particular family member: the child. As we have seen, the one-child policy in China creates tension for Chinese parents, and for moms in particular. This often translates into a heightened sense of concern about everything to do with the health of their child. As one team member stated, "There are not many second chance parents in China." Filial relationships being what they are, it is safe to say that Chinese parents are to a degree obsessed with the future of their children.

"Let Kids Discover and Explore the World."

The core question for the Safeguard team became: "How can we develop this strategy to be in tune with the deeper emotions, concerns, and feelings of Chinese moms?" The agency team spent much of 2000 and 2001 on an Xploring exercise throughout China. The team played with children, talked to moms, visited their homes. Moms said they wanted to let their kids be kids, play in the dirt, skin their knees and do the things kids are supposed to do, but they were cautious because they knew that their kids could ultimately get sick, which could put their child behind the other kids, threatening their dreams.

Safeguard's product attributes were perfect for resolving moms' conflicted minds. The new message would be as relevant as a message could be. Safeguard's germ protection meant that kids could be kids and still protect themselves. Mom could have the best of both worlds for her child.

This led to the "Let Kids Discover and Explore the World" campaign. Safeguard's television commercials for this approach were straightforward, letting moms know they should not be afraid to let their children go out and discover the world around them, as long as they made sure to wash away the germs and impurities. How successful was this approach? The campaign doubled Safeguard's already sizable share of the bar soap category.

Beyond Exploration

By 2007, China's moms had developed a more balanced attitude towards their children and the outside world—in part due to Safeguard. So P&G modified their approach. A television commercial indicative of the new approach was called "Sand." It featured a young boy playing in the sand. As he runs his hands through it, he realizes that if he were to add water, it would firm up, allowing him to mold it. The voiceover tells the viewer: "When kids use their hands, they are using their brain." By the end of the commercial, the little boy has built a sand pyramid that dwarfs both his friends and him.

Beyond the focus on children using their brain as well as their hands, this campaign also emphasizes that freedom from germs means children will have fewer sick days, missing less school, and missing out on fewer opportunities to learn. These were things moms still cared about.

When kids use their hands,
they are using their brain

The powerful insights the team gathered from their Xploring trips made the development of the creative ideas—like the "Sand" commercial—relatively easy. This is a common theme around Lovemarks. Great emotional insights seem to turn on a light that guides the way creatively. According to Ann Jingco, the regional account head for Safeguard in Asia, "Creative development was so fast. We had so many ideas that we had trouble figuring out which ones to present. Our clients had the same issue. They liked so many of the ideas, it was hard to decide which ones to approve."

According to Laura Xiong, P&G's category vice president for Greater China,

舒肤佳 为妈妈保护明日冠军而自豪

Safeguard, proud protector of mom's playground champion

"This advertising really resonates with moms. And it is important for single children, who are kept very busy, and might otherwise not be allowed to play around outside, which is so important for their development and self-esteem. Moms no longer feel the need to say, 'Don't do that!' or 'Don't touch that!'"

....

The campaign has a number of digital angles too. Two recent campaigns used the web and social networking to full advantage. For the brand's 20th anniversary in China in 2011, Safeguard avoided the usual self-congratulatory advertising and instead used it as an opportunity to rally young adults to thank their mom for providing a healthy and happy childhood. The brand provided a website where people could send their mom a thank you card by email. Over a seven-week period 9.5 million people participated on the site. In 2012, to help celebrate the London Olympic games, Safeguard introduced "Playground Champions." The idea is to encourage kids to fulfill their athletic potential on the playground. The centerpiece is the "Safeguard Playground Championship," a playground Olympics for kids throughout China with participation driven through social media, websites, blogs, and point of purchase messaging.

"The ones

Safeguarding the Ones You Love

Safeguard's efforts in China and other developing markets go way beyond the desire to sell soap. The brand takes upon itself the serious task of helping to improve the health of the people. Part of this task is education. In communities around China, Safeguard educates children—to date over 39 million of them—on the importance of washing hands. One way they teach children how to wash their hands, properly and thoroughly, is with the help of a catchy little tune complete with lyrics about rubbing one hand over the other and sliding fingers together. Aside from education, the brand works to help deliver clean water to rural communities throughout China.

Due to Safeguard's salience in working to improve good health, government bodies often partner with it. They know that washing hands is serious business helping ensure better health in the developing world. For example, Safeguard was approached by the Chinese government in the mid-2000s to help respond to the SARS epidemic.

In the Philippines, it was approached by UNICEF to help put up water facilities in areas where water was needed. The Philippine minister for health, Juan Flavier, even appeared in Safeguard commercials, figuring that the brand had the same vision as his ministry, and could work together with them to help the ministry's message be more effective. The brand team likens this to the "institutionalization" of the brand. In the words of Aziz Jindani, global marketing director on Safeguard, "Soaps are soaps, but Safeguard is something significantly more." He likens it to a family's "everyday insurance policy."

That better health is at the core of what Safeguard is all about is clear from watching internal films that P&G creates to define its equity and purpose for its employees. The films emphasize the "small, but meaningful changes" the brand helps create to protect people's "fundamental right to health." Overall, they see the brand as "helping people safeguard the ones they love." Again, as we have seen with so many cases in this book, the emphasis is on love. Before any consideration of sales, Safeguard has a real and abiding concern for the people who buy it.

you love"

The genuine concern for improved health is echoed by the people who work on the brand. When interviewed, they were asked what they were most proud of. No one talked about sales or share or brand metrics. Ann Jingco said,

"We are helping kids; teaching them how to wash their hands. We are helping moms. We are saving lives. I get goosebumps just thinking about being part of this."

Neel Chaurasia, global brand agency leader for Safeguard at Saatchi, had a similar response: "I am Asian, and I know that something as simple as hand washing can save lives. An infectious disease can be prevented by just one incident of hand washing… Safeguard is a brand with a meaningful purpose, and I am proud to work on it. This is not about selling soap. It is much more." These responses go to the heart of what P&G aspires to achieve for all of its brands, or in the company's parlance: "purpose-inspired brand building."

Planners often talk about strategy as a process of "laddering." They build a communication ladder where each rung leads the consumer from the product's attributes to its benefits to its higher-order emotional appeals. The development of today's Safeguard strategy was over a decade in the making. The planners built the strongest ladder possible from the product's general anti-bacterial function in the 1990s, to the focus on letting children explore and learn from the world around them today.

Today Safeguard is very much a movement led by Chinese moms. The first stage of the movement is when they realize that good hygiene is important for their child. The second stage is when they realize it is good for all the children of China. The third stage is when they actively support and proselytize the message.

The emotional attachment of moms to Safeguard jumps out in research responses. When reading them it is almost hard to believe that they are talking about soap. Moms say things like:

"Without Safeguard my life is incomplete. We are not 100% protected."

"Without Safeguard there would be chaos in our house."

"I grew up with Safeguard."

China is the world's largest potential market, but this campaign is having an impact all across the globe. The campaign is appearing in various forms in India, Pakistan, Latin America, parts of Africa, and as we have seen, the Philippines. In Pakistan, where 250,000 children a year become victims of diarrhea, a Safeguard TV spot was deemed to be in the public good and aired as a public service message.

Results

Today, Safeguard's share of the bar soap market in China stands at over 50% in a country of over 1.3 billion people. Safeguard's bodywash is number one and growing. The number of households using Safeguard in China is more than the combined population of nine countries in Europe (France, Italy, Sweden, Spain, Holland, Greece, Switzerland, Austria, Portugal). How much soap is that? The number of Safeguard bars sold in China in a year could encircle the globe.

The Team at P&G gave this award to their counterparts at Saatchi & Saatchi for "Turning everything to gold"

As with most Lovemarks, Safeguard also commands a premium price in a category where commodity pricing is the norm. Safeguard is worth more because it is much more than just a bar of soap.

Laura Xiong highlighted a fascinating aspect of the brand's success: "In China, one of three bars of Safeguard sold is a cheaper-priced counterfeit product. However, when we make the packaging differentiation very clear between the counterfeit and the real product, people gladly pay more for the real thing. Our efforts here are really working to reduce the number of counterfeits sold."

The Safeguard campaign has won many awards. In addition to advertising industry kudos, the team has garnered a range of impressive awards. Among them: the Red Cross Philanthropist Award, the China Government Volunteer Award, the Saatchi & Saatchi "Nothing is Impossible" Award, the China Best Advertiser Award, and Procter & Gamble's President's Award. Perhaps most special to the team at Saatchi was when their counterparts at P&G designed a special award called the "Midas of Safeguard Award." The award celebrated the spirit of their commitment to "Safeguard the One You Love," which turned everything to gold.

Aziz Jindani has worked on Safeguard for over seven years. He calls the advertising developed by Saatchi a "great" campaign. He says, "What makes it great is that it is unlike almost any other product. The benefit is invisible. You cannot see the bacteria being washed away. There is no other way to communicate this than through Lovemarks, and the language of love and trust."

The Safeguard team even has a mantra:

"When we think like a bar of soap, we are one. When we think like a caregiver, a protector, and a Lovemark, we are something greater, more meaningful, and beyond price comparison."

Enough said.

Memories Bring You Back to The Ritz-Carlton

Memories elicit some of our strongest emotions, the most intense of which often come from our travels. The Ritz-Carlton Hotel Company has a deep understanding of the role each of their employees plays in making great memories, whether the guest is staying alone for business or with their family on vacation.

Perhaps no other company in the world does more to invest in its people, and work with them to build memorable experiences for their customers. The Ritz-Carlton motto, "Ladies and Gentlemen Serving Ladies and Gentlemen," captures the high value the company puts both on its guests and its staff. A stated corporate goal for each employee is to "anticipate and fulfill each guest's needs." Much of The Ritz-Carlton's mystique comes from their uncanny ability to do just that. The ladies and gentlemen of The Ritz-Carlton are given great latitude to make every stay memorable. For example, every single staff member is authorized to spend—without approval from their general manager—up to $2,000 on a guest if they deem it necessary to improve service or solve a problem.

This dedication to service leads to some great stories, and storytelling is core to The Ritz-Carlton's ethos. Every day, every one of their 35,000 employees worldwide gathers locally for a 15-minute meeting known as the "Line-up." In this meeting they review guest experiences, discuss guest issues, and celebrate great feats of service by telling a "wow story" about how one of their staff did something amazing to make a guest's stay special. The Line-ups are done on a department-by-department basis, for every shift. The average Ritz-Carlton hotel might have upwards of 25 Line-ups a day.

A typical wow story comes from The Ritz-Carlton in Bali. A family had brought with them specialized eggs and milk due to their son's food allergies. Unfortunately, the milk had soured and the eggs had broken in transit. The Ritz-Carlton staff searched the town but could not find the right milk and eggs to replace them. The executive chef, however, remembered a store in Singapore that sold them. He contacted his mother-in-law, who bought the products and had them flown to Bali at no cost to the guests. Now that's service.

The Ritz-Carlton's corporate offices receive a consistent stream of personal letters from guests bringing wow stories to the company's attention, along with the name of the staff member who created such a special experience. It is not unusual for the guest to call out not just one but many staff members who all contributed to their special stay. A recent letter from a guest at The Ritz-Carlton in Westchester, New York gave accolades to: "The doorman, Gary…Jackie, the pastry chef…Justin, the ballroom captain…Oscar, Justin's assistant…Cecile, the spa supervisor… and the resourceful Ellen Kohler." The fact that a single guest felt indebted to so many people says a lot about The Ritz-Carlton. The fact that they could actually remember all of their names says volumes.

Julie Michael, who is the executive director on the account at Saatchi & Saatchi's Team One agency in Los Angeles, got to experience a wow story first hand on a recent business trip to Shanghai to attend a Ritz-Carlton conference. During the trip, her husband became seriously ill with a gastro-intestinal ailment. Not content to just stick the couple in a cab, the hotel's staff hand-delivered them to the hospital and stayed to translate all their communications with doctors and staff.

The wow stories told by Ritz-Carlton employees in the Line-up, day after day, bring their mission into sharp focus. They spark new ideas for service, and create a sense of palpable success and pride. The stories are inspirational because they are real, and they happen every day at Ritz-Carlton hotels worldwide. As Julie Michael put it, "We read these things and write about these things, but when you experience them first hand you are just blown away, and in the case of my husband and myself, incredibly thankful."

When The Ritz-Carlton and Team One thought about ways to leverage the memories created for the hotel's guests, they expressed it as a twist on the banal line "Please Stay with Us." The new thought was an inversion of that idea, namely, "Let Us Stay with You." It was quintessential Lovemarks thinking: putting the brand in the context of the consumer.

The idea was much more than a word twist. It was the fruition of comprehensive analysis into the affluent hotel market and its customers. Team One enshrined their findings in a presentation called "Understanding the Global Affluent Tribe." It described a group, or "tribe," of affluent consumers who travel the world spending $500-plus on hotel rooms per night, noting they often have more in common with each other (regardless of country of origin) than with people who may live near them. They are bonded by what they love versus where they live. Great hotels like The Ritz-Carlton become surrogate homes. Five commonalities were identified as deep preoccupations of the Global Affluent Tribe:

Mobility: *Life is comprised of a series of self-discoveries.*

Success: *Creativity and talent are more impressive than inheritance or pedigree.*

Status: *Knowledge and connoisseurship have high value.*

Networking: *Having access to connecting with other like-minded people matters.*

Consumption: *Purposeful and meaningful consumption beats wasteful consumption.*

An example of the "Let Us Stay with You" print campaign, inviting people to let The Ritz-Carlton make their stay more memorable

For potential guests, the ads in the campaign spark dozens of ideas on how Ritz-Carlton's staff can make your stay more memorable, including:

"Let us turn your nine-year old into a sous chef."

"Let us invent a drink in your honor."

"Let us re-create the recipe from your favorite meal in Paris."

"Let us start each meeting with your client's favorite orchids."

"Let us make you captain of your very own ship."

The campaign also featured a series of online videos, called "Art of the Craft," dedicated to the specific points of expertise of Ritz-Carlton employees that allow them to make great memories. In one, we meet Ian Cauble, sommelier at The Ritz-Carlton at Half Moon Bay in Northern California. In order to learn about the wines he serves, he makes visits to the vineyards where the grapes are grown. We even see him getting down into the dirt to understand how the soil impacts the flavor of the wine. He tells us:

Mark Miller, chief strategy officer at Team One, believes that transforming brands into experiences is an example of the new luxury economy, whether you are talking about small luxuries like Starbucks coffee or shopping in Whole Foods, or big luxuries like spending the night at a luxury hotel. Turning experiences into memories is even higher ground. Of the new campaign, he says, "'Let Us Stay with You' changes the equation from measuring your stay in number of days to number of memories. It is about getting your memory's worth, not just your money's worth. That's the difference between a passive relationship with your hotel, which is what happens on-site for a finite period of time, and an active relationship which endures before, during, and after your stay."

"Every bottle of wine has a unique story and reason why it tastes the way it does. If a sommelier can share those stories and bring more meaning to what's in your glass, I think they are doing their job."

Ian Cauble demonstrates
"The Art of the Craft"

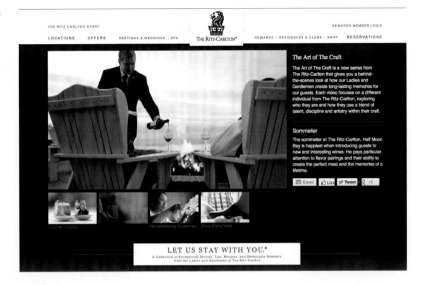

Nicole LaValette, The Ritz-Carlton's director of sales and marketing in New York, underscored the importance of the "Art of the Craft" stories. She said, "Today's travelers are very sophisticated. They want to know the stories behind the experiences. They have inquiring minds. The stories make the experiences, and them, more interesting."

Global Impact

The brand's communication platform is truly global. It comes to life in China, Japan, the Middle East, and Europe as well as the US. In Japan, for example, The Ritz-Carlton and Team One partnered with Japan's highly-regarded *Nile Magazine* to bring the guest perspective to life through a series of portraits taken by famous local photographers.

The images captured beloved memories of each guest, whether a one-of-a-kind travel experience or special time spent with a loved one, while using the brand's hotels in Tokyo, Osaka, and Okinawa as backdrops. The images will appear in *Nile*'s print editorial and digital formats as well as a special live exhibition.

In China, which will become the world's number one outbound market by 2015, the campaign will soon have strong social media and mobile elements, in a country where most internet users have leap-frogged desktops and use mobile phones as their primary digital connection devices. The Ritz-Carlton and Team One are also pursuing customized, Mandarin-only broadcast and video ideas, including documentary and reality-style television programming. On the product side of the equation, The Ritz-Carlton Shanghai, Pudong was named the number one hotel in the world in *Condé Nast Traveler*'s 2011 Readers Choice Awards.

"Let Us Stay with You"

The team knew they were on to something really special when, on the campaign's launch day, they attended a Line-up in the 100-degree laundry room of The Ritz-Carlton Laguna Niguel in southern California. In the words of Team One's Nick Teare, who had come to the laundry room after spending almost two hours making a presentation to visiting Marriott executives about the brand and the new campaign, "Many of the housekeeping staff said that the campaign gave them additional pride in their work, and pride in a company that was willing to tell 'their story' to the world." The campaign was not advertising artifice; it was a reflection of reality. He was particularly pleased when the Line-up ended with Matt Helm, director of housekeeping at the hotel, explaining what "Let Us Stay with You" meant to him. As Teare put it with a smile, "He did the same thing, in five minutes, more beautifully and eloquently than I had in two hours."

A Campaign that Improves Operations

The Ritz-Carlton's president and chief operating officer, Herve Humler, sees "Let Us Stay with You" as much more than an advertising campaign. He notes, "It is a marketing platform that has become an operating platform." The hotel group has three steps of service, which are sacrosanct: 1) A warm and sincere greeting using the guest's name; 2) anticipation and fulfillment of each guest's needs; and 3) a fond farewell. About a year and a half ago, Humler started talking about a potential fourth step: emotional engagement. He said: "We were talking about it, but did not know how to define it. 'Let Us Stay with You' is the perfect articulation. This is not a short-term campaign. It is what we do and who we are. It will define the fourth step of our service vision: delivering memories." He calls it a "springboard" for the brand's future.

The campaign idea encourages the ladies and gentlemen of The Ritz-Carlton to go beyond watching guests and to start observing them, perceiving patterns that will help them meet unrecognized needs better than ever. Such needs are not always a big "wow." More often, it is a series of small but personal gestures that add to the mystery and sensuality of how the brand operates: just the right mix of a half caf/half decaf or a foreign-language newspaper or a surprise photo of a family pet in your guest room.

Making a business stay more memorable in Russia

Scott Geraghty, general manager of The Ritz-Carlton on New York's Central Park, echoed Humler's thoughts:

"'Let Us Stay with You' resonates well with our culture. It works at a very personal level. The thought captures the service delivery that each one of us strives to deliver every day in this hotel."

....

The results so far have been outstanding, especially for a luxury brand in challenging economic times. According to the brand's tracking study, The Ritz-Carlton has reestablished itself as the "1st Choice Preference" in the category, beating rival Four Seasons. It has had 12 months of share growth and successive years of double-digit growth in revenue per available room (RevPAR), which is the ultimate measure of hotel financial success. The Ritz-Carlton commands a strong premium for their product even during the recession. They are shattering the traditional price/value equation. The focus for their customers is not dollar cost, but whether the experience was "worth it."

The advertising campaign has been featured in a *New York Times* article and has received over $33 million in free publicity.

The Ritz-Carlton is a different kind of Lovemark. As a service brand, its primary focus is to emotionally inspire its staff, who in turn will be motivated to make every guest's experience a memorable one. The "Let Us Stay with You" campaign does that memorably.

Team One's Julie Michael captured the essence of the Lovemark idea: "Asking to be let into people's memories is even more personal than asking to be let into their lives. If Lovemarks are about intimacy, then this is as intimate as you can get."

Like Safeguard, where the reality of the brand was much more than a small bar of soap, a stay at The Ritz-Carlton is much more than a fine bed, a great shower, or a first-class meal.

The Ritz-Carlton is about worth versus value, and about emotional fulfillment beyond rationality. It equates to higher margins, more demand, and loyalty beyond reason.

♥

08

Forging Relationships 08

This chapter features case stories for Miller High Life and Toyota 4X4s. The common ground for these stories is their ability to understand what makes their core users different from others, and how to plumb those differences to speak to the hearts of users and non-users alike. Each brand did more than mimic their best customers. They got to the heart of what made core users feel unique, and the values that differentiated them. In these cases, the brands became one with their most important audiences.

Miller High Life: The Rebirth of an American Icon

In March of 2010, Joe Abegg was sitting in a huge Las Vegas conference center with about 5,000 people. It was the MillerCoors National Distributor Meeting. As brand manager for Miller High Life beer, Joe was both nervous and excited.

He was nervous because distributor meetings are the place you share your new marketing plans and advertising campaigns for the upcoming year with your superiors, your colleagues, and most importantly, the thousands of distributors who sell the beer to retailers, who then sell to consumers. You get one chance to wow them. He was excited, because he was about to put forward an idea he deeply believed in, an idea that everyone would remember long after the convention was over. High Life wasn't MillerCoors's biggest brand, but it would be the one everyone talked about later.

The lights went down and MillerCoors's chief marketing officer, Andy England, went on stage to introduce Paul Rieckhoff, the head of the Iraq and Afghanistan Veterans of America (IAVA). He talked about Miller High Life's sponsorship of a program to welcome back Iraq and Afghanistan veterans. The program was called "Give a Vet a Piece of the High Life."

For every High Life cap or tab people collected, MillerCoors would donate 10 cents toward "High Life Experiences" for returning vets. Over $1,000,000 per year would go toward paying former soldiers' way into sporting events, concerts, outdoor adventures, and other fun experiences, to help give them a chance to "live the high life," and remind them how appreciative Americans are for their service. In a typical experience, a group of veterans and their families would attend a major league baseball game and be recognized on the field. As Rieckhoff said, the recognition is really incredible "because we didn't have ticker tape parades when we came home." The presentation ended with a commercial that had been developed to support the program.

When the commercial was over, people in the audience who had served in the military were asked to stand and be recognized. Distributors are a famously hard-nosed audience; many of them now had tears in their eyes.

Abegg had always believed that the idea was more than a promotion; he called it a "movement," where High Life would rally its drinkers to make sure veterans got the welcome home they deserved. He knew it would succeed when the distributors gave Rieckhoff's speech not one, but four standing ovations. The distributors were so fired up, and there was so much interest to be part of it, that the first thing the team needed to do was go back and re-work all of the program's financials.

Even before the distributor meeting, the agency team had shared the campaign with consumers in focus groups. After seeing it, two men in the groups said they had served. They were teary eyed and their voices slightly choked up.

How could a brand that was floundering less than 10 years ago be seen as having the right, and the undeniable authenticity, to welcome home veterans for all of America? By reinventing a lost brand and reclaiming the love it had fostered for earlier generations.

An American Icon Falters

Before we look at where Miller High Life is now, it helps to know where it has been. The product was first sold in 1903: it is Miller's oldest brand. It was the forerunner of the modern American lager beer. High Life was famous for its quality, its clear bottle, its famous slogan "The Champagne of Bottle Beers," and its iconic image of a woman sitting on the moon. High Life also had a longstanding relationship with the military. It supplied its beer to the troops during World War II, and the girl-in-the-moon logo could even be seen painted on the nose cones of fighter planes.

The Miller High Life
"Girl in the Moon"

By 1979, Miller High Life was the number-two brand in the US after Budweiser. The next few decades were not kind to High Life, however. Budweiser entrenched its number one position. Light beers carved out big market share. Imported and microbrewery beers grew by leaps and bounds. Miller also innovated with big new brands that did not bear the High Life moniker, like Miller Genuine Draft. The result was that by the early 2000s, High Life was a nearly forgotten brand with low market share, a brand that was sold primarily on price.

The Miller High Life Delivery Man

In 2007, Miller and their agency at the time, Crispin Porter + Bogusky, introduced a new campaign for High Life featuring a beer delivery man, played by an actor named Windell Middlebrooks. The character had blue-collar values, and instead of delivering beer, the audience saw him removing beer from places where people were being extravagant. In one commercial, for example, he removed the High Life from a bar that has a $20 cover charge.

Soon afterwards, Saatchi & Saatchi New York won the High Life account. They realized right away that Windell's character had a lot going for it, but they gave it a strategic twist. One of the first things the agency did after winning the account was talk to High Life consumers—men 28–35 who drink 6–8 domestic beers a week. They loved Windell, but they did not have a grudge against people who had money or who wanted to spend a little extra money to have a good time.

What they did hate was pretense. So Saatchi redefined what Windell's character was all about. He would be about common sense, and Miller High Life would become "common sense in a bottle." One of the first commercials created by Saatchi showed Windell entering a luxury skybox at a baseball game. He did not remove the beer because the people were wealthy; he removed it because they were being pretentious. They were socializing and not watching the game; they did not even know what inning the game was in. After removing the beer, Windell joined a crowd of "real fans" in the bleachers for a beer and hot dogs. Brendan Noonan, who is the current brand manager on High Life, likens this last scene to a Robin Hood moment: "The people in the skybox are paying more to have less fun. That makes no sense! So we are returning the High Life to the people."

The combination of the right strategy and Windell's undeniable charm started to get Miller High Life noticed again. According to Noonan,

"We saw three years of straight growth, which is rare for a beer brand that has had such a long period of decline. When we tested the actual commercials, the scores for awareness and persuasion were off the charts."

....

Windell takes on pretension in a luxury skybox

The One-Second Ad

Now that High Life, its values, and key character were established, the objective was to get the most impact for what was now a smaller brand with a modest budget. The Miller High Life brand team and the Saatchi team were up to the task. They came up with something that would prove what High Life was all about on the biggest stage possible. Better yet, it was something that had never been done before.

Here's how it worked:

Perhaps nothing in the world leads to more advertiser pretention than the Super Bowl. Big name brands routinely plunk down $3 million for a 30-second spot and often spend upwards of $2 million more to produce over-the-top commercials shot by world famous directors, using the most expensive computer graphics. And many Super Bowl commercials are for High Life's direct competitors.

The agency asked itself, "What would High Life and Windell think of all this pretension?" The answer was obvious. In fact, in the days after the 2008 Super Bowl, High Life ran an ad where Windell told the other deliverymen just what he thought of the ridiculously expensive and sometimes stupid ads.

This led to a breakthrough advertising idea. What if High Life showed up the big spenders, and instead of buying 30 seconds for $3 million plus, they bought a one-second ad instead? What if High Life could get the same value in one second that the big boys got in 30 seconds?

The idea was outrageous, in large part because nothing like it had ever been imagined, much less seriously discussed. The list of problems was endless, but two questions stood out:

1) **Would anyone sell them a one-second ad on the Super Bowl?**

2) **Could they communicate anything at all in one second, or would it just be a gimmick, a wasted subliminal blip?**

....

The conventional answer to question number one was "doubtful." The conventional answer to question number two was "probably not." But the team was undaunted. Embracing Saatchi & Saatchi's motto of "Nothing is Impossible," they tenaciously pursued the idea and knocked off the problems one by one in partnership with Miller's other marketing partners, such as their PR agency and their below-the-line agency.

From a media perspective, NBC, the network running the broadcast, would not sell them a one-second ad. In fact, the network would not sell them an ad at all given Anheuser-Busch's exclusive rights to advertise beer on the Super Bowl broadcast. The Saatchi media team then approached the Owned-and-Operated stations (known as "O-and-Os") that would be running the game regionally. They agreed. That is, they agreed until a top executive at NBC Sports asked the O-and-Os to cease and desist from selling the space to High Life. Not surprisingly, they rescinded their offers. Undeterred, the media team put together a package of scores of local stations in key markets that would be carrying the game. Even those stations would not sell them a one-second ad, so they bought a five-second ad and left a few seconds of blank space before and after the ad.

The Miller one-second Super Bowl ad

But what about the message itself? Could a one-second ad really be remembered?

The Miller/Saatchi team had three great things going for them. First, they realized that the novelty of the one-second ad had the potential to make this a publicity bonanza. With enough coverage of this unique idea before the game, they could have viewers glued to the set waiting for it, and hoping not to miss such a short, unique cultural moment. Second, they had a loved icon in their delivery man, Windell. He had high awareness and would act as a mnemonic device, giving them the chance to make a single second very memorable. Third, they had the internet, which, if used properly, could give the one-second idea life before, during, and after the big game.

There was another consideration that favored High Life's approach. According to Connor Bryant, the brand's account director at Saatchi New York, "We were in the midst of a deep recession. The headlines in 2008 were all about people losing their homes and jobs. For our competitors to spend over $25 million in total to run ads and have beer category exclusivity on the Super Bowl was somewhat grotesque."

Super Bowl XLIII between the Pittsburgh Steelers and the Arizona Cardinals was scheduled to take place on February 1, 2009 in Tampa, Florida. There would be a sellout crowd in the stadium of over 70,000 people and a total TV audience of over 150 million people, many of whom would see the ad.

"We were living the High Life positioning. No pretense, just getting it done."

Prior to the game, Saatchi and Miller scored a coup. *Tonight Show* host Jay Leno was so intrigued by the idea that he invited Windell Middlebrooks to come on to the show the week before the Super Bowl to talk about it. Now millions of people would be primed and on the lookout. The *Tonight Show* appearance also primed the pumps of other media, significantly increasing the number of stories online and in the press.

Miller even created a dedicated website (www.1SecondAd.com) where people could see the seventy-plus one-second ads that were actually shot and try to figure out which one would be used during the game.

The website also included other High Life commercials and, for fun, showed visitors what $3 million would actually buy in the real world, like one million pounds or so of bacon.

The commercial ran as scheduled and it was an instant hit. The version that ran was Windell looking at camera and saying "High Life!" There was a ton of positive buzz on the web, in the media, and on Miller's Facebook page. The total value of additional free publicity was pegged at over $2 million, or almost enough to buy a :30 Super Bowl spot outright.

According to Saatchi's Nick Miaritis, who was the account director on the campaign:

"Lack of timing was our best asset. We had three weeks to plan, produce, post-produce, and ship the ads, and a shoestring budget compared to the other Super Bowl advertisers. I remember, we were in this abandoned warehouse in Brooklyn with rats running around and no director. We didn't care. We just got on with it. We shot dozens upon dozens of great takes. Windell was amazing! We were living the High Life positioning. No pretense, just getting it done."

Miller gets behind unpretentious small business owners like Del's Barber Shop

Super Bowl: Take Two

One of the most daunting tasks in marketing is to follow up on a huge success. After all, running a one-second ad is a brilliant idea, but it only works once.

In 2010, Saatchi proposed another Super Bowl idea, but this time they would buy a full 30-second commercial. How could they do this while still remaining true to their common sense, anti-pretension ethos?

They did it by donating the spot to hardworking small business owners. What better way to highlight High Life's positioning than to help small business owners during the height of a recession? The idea was called "Little Guys on the Big Game."

The spot featured the High Life delivery man introducing the owners of four small businesses from around the United States: Del's Barber Shop in Escondido, California; Tim's Baseball Card Shop in Chicago, Illinois; Loretta's Authentic Pralines in New Orleans, Louisiana; Bizarre Guitar & Drum in Phoenix, Arizona.

These were down-to-earth, no-nonsense business owners. Loretta Harrison of Loretta's Authentic Pralines, for example, salvaged her company—the first African-American-owned candy company in New Orleans—after it was almost destroyed by Hurricane Katrina. In speaking about Bob Turner, who owned Bizarre Guitar & Drum in Phoenix, Joe Abegg—who has since been promoted to director of category management at MillerCoors—said, "We came across a guy who started his own business and worked his way up. It was all about his non-pretentious, no-BS attitude, and that fits our brand values."

When Turner received a call from Miller telling him he had a chance to be in a Super Bowl commercial, he was dubious. "I kept thinking they were trying to steal my ID," he said. "It's so far-fetched they would pick a guy in Phoenix, Arizona, with a little guitar store."

The High Life

Miller High Life is now a brand that punches well above its weight. Between 2009 and 2011 High Life's advertising budget was cut significantly, yet the brand's health metrics have never been stronger. For example, High Life leads its competitive set in response to the following statements:

"Is a beer for someone like me."

"Has strong heritage and tradition."

"Worth what you pay for it."

"High quality."

As Abegg noted, "We got more sell in, more ads and more case displays in supermarkets than we should have. And even as a sub-premium beer, we were able to modestly increase our price." That in a nutshell is the business definition of consumer loyalty beyond reason.

By the time Abegg and his team showed the Iraq and Afghanistan Veterans of America (IAVA) campaign to their distributors, a lot had already been done to reestablish Miller High Life as a vibrant brand, a brand for common sense people who wanted a great beer at a reasonable price.

The brand's history, combined with its renewed vibrancy, made it the perfect brand to stand up for veterans and rally Americans to collect bottle caps in their honor. In bars across America one can still see large plastic Miller High Life bottles that act as receptacles for thousands of bottle caps that will be turned in at 10 cents apiece to help make a veteran feel welcomed home. According to Noonan, "People get that the Vets gave up their 'high life' moments so we could have them instead. And the distributors are prouder of this campaign than anything, not just because it sells beer, but because it is the right thing to do."

And no one disputes that High Life is in a position once again to do this for America.

is Back

As we have seen, Joe Abegg and his team described this campaign as a "movement" rather than a promotion. Lovemarks are just that, movements that consumers choose to join. A look at just one of the letters they received from a thankful vet makes it clear that this movement was a very successful one:

"I want to thank the IAVA, Miller Brewing Company, and all the other sponsors that provide veterans with these rewards. I retired from the Army 31 August 2009. My final deployment to Iraq was a 16 month tour that spanned all of 2007 and part of 2008. I am married and have 5 boys. My youngest son was 3 years old when I returned to Iraq from my mid-tour leave. I will never forget that day. As my wife and boys dropped me off at the airport my wife and children were crying and my youngest cried out don't leave me daddy. He then begged my wife not to leave me at the airport. I promised him and my other boys I would retire as soon as I returned home from Iraq, which I did.

"As I look back over my career I have left my family many times over the years, but that moment when I looked into my boys' eyes and could see the depth of their heartache, well that was the moment I realized it was not only I that made sacrifices for our nation. I knew it was time to hang up the dog tags and be the husband and father they deserved to have. I was reminded of that moment this past Friday night as my youngest son, now five years old, cheered and gave out high fives to everyone sitting close by as the White Sox won the game. He then told me how much he loved being there and it was the best weekend ever.

"I know this letter is rather long, but I felt compelled to let the IAVA, Sponsors, and fellow Americans know how grateful my son and I are for the opportunity to enjoy some much needed father and son time at the White Sox game. I want everyone to know these rewards are not just another check the block program. These programs not only give veterans an opportunity to relax and have a good time, but they are a reminder that we are not alone and reaffirmation to our loved ones that their sacrifices did not go unnoticed."

Respectfully
Julian C. Nicholson
U.S. Army Retired

AUSTRALIA BORDER SECURITY CASE STORY

Toyota Secures Australia's Borders

Miller forged a new relationship with their drinkers by understanding their unpretentious, no-nonsense attitude. In Australia, Toyota similarly connected with demanding drivers in the unforgiving Aussie outback, and in the process reestablished the Lovemark status of Toyota 4X4 trucks with their historical core audience.

For decades Toyota held the leadership position in rural Australia, built on the success of tough 4X4 trucks like the Toyota Hilux, Land Cruiser, and Prado. By 2009, however, with the growth of Australia's city populations, a global financial crisis affecting advertising budgets, and a model lineup that was the largest in Australia, Toyota was not talking to rural customers as frequently or forcefully about 4X4s as they once had.

Rural Australia had always been a very loyal customer base for Toyota, and a strong influence on why all Australians—country or city—had an affinity with the brand. Yet for a number of years Toyota had not communicated directly to this group. They had advertised to them, a lot, but had not produced a piece of communication that was aimed at connecting (in this case reconnecting) specifically with them and their unique needs and outlook.

The target audience was "true blue outback blokes." Saatchi & Saatchi Australia used insights from their years of Xploring in the outback to define what made this group of guys unique. Some of the most piercing insights were:

• The outback is a bloody tough environment.

• These guys would never swap their jobs for a job in the city.

• To them, reliability has a real meaning because it can be genuinely life threatening if your truck breaks down in the outback.

• They believe that Australia, in general, is "getting soft."

• They believe that Toyota understands them.

• They have always appreciated Toyota's honest, entertaining, not-taking-things-too-seriously approach. In other words, Toyota has never been afraid of "taking the piss" (Australian for "making fun of things") just like them.

• Worryingly, however, they felt that Toyota had "not done anything good for a while," in terms of communication meaningful to them.

Saatchi Australia developed a campaign to get right to the core of what outback blokes had been missing from Toyota. The campaign was developed to a creative proposition that stated, "Real hard cars for hard places." It would make fun (er, take the piss) of Australia "getting soft." In doing so, it would make a point to this target that Toyota still got them, and was still making the tough, reliable, dependable vehicles they always had.

The idea that came out of the proposition was the "Country Australia Border Crossing" campaign. The advertising dramatized a border security zone for a tough, no-nonsense country where "nothing soft" would be allowed in.

The campaign featured TV, print, point of sale, and digital elements. In the launch 60-second TV spot, we see a border patrol in action replete with an intimidating array of helicopters, four-wheel drives and German Shepherds. The captain of the guards tells us:

Country Australia Border Patrol keeps a vigilant lookout for anything that is not tough enough, like pretender four-wheel drives

"It's a hard country, and we want to keep it that way. Nothing soft gets in. City people don't know what the hell they are facing out here."

Various guards are warning people to put their preppy shirt collars down or to put down their hair dryers.

The guards are confiscating precious little dogs. In a parody of a drunk-driving stop, they ask people when they had their last latte. They arrest a man for trying to smuggle in tofu packed up to look like illicit drugs. They are even catching drivers who are putting fake Toyota badges on their cars in an effort to trick the patrol into thinking their car is tough enough to take the outback. This last bit was a nod to 4WD Toyota-pretender vehicles that don't have the brand's toughness or heritage, which the company jokingly calls "soft-roaders."

This print ad shows some of the items "prohibited" in the outback

NOTHING SOFT GETS IN

The tone of the whole commercial is deadly serious with tongue planted firmly in cheek. The underlying message is clear though. There is a not so fine line between the city and the country in Australia, and it is defined by the tenacity of the people and Toyota's tough 4X4s.

Toyota's rural dealers knew right away that this would speak to their customers because, as outback people, it spoke to them. They did what any good dealers would: they had border patrol uniforms made for their salespeople, and put up warning posters in their showrooms listing prohibited items, such as "manbags," energy drinks, and croissants.

Scott Thompson, Toyota Australia's division manager for marketing, noted that the campaign led to an almost endless extension of ideas: "Saatchi was back almost every day with an extension of the idea into PR, direct marketing, merchandising, etc. That's the hallmark of a really good idea." In a tip of the hat to the outback, he likened it to "a creek that just flows and flows."

The people of the outback loved the campaign and rewarded Toyota for reconnecting with them. Toyota regularly measures "desirability" for their models, and desirability for Prado, Land Cruiser, and Hilux all increased. In just the first three months of the campaign's launch period, Toyota experienced extraordinary sales results, which were particularly impressive given the effects of the global financial crisis. Land Cruiser's core 200 model had a sales increase of 44%. Hilux 4X4 sales rose 61%. Hilux 4X2 sales followed with a lift of 58%, while Prado sales rose 21%.

The sales lift was not just in rural areas. The ad was shown in the metro markets during the Australian Rules Football Grand Final. It was a huge hit. Because city-Australians see the outback as their heritage, and a place that reflects the true spirit of their country, they loved the campaign too, and did not mind the joke at their expense. Self-deprecation is a key facet of the Australian character, and Toyota understood that.

According to Thompson, the original brief to the agency was for two campaigns, one for the country market and one for the city market, but this campaign worked for both, so only one campaign was needed.

The campaign won five gold Lions at Cannes, the most coveted prize in advertising. Winning one gold would make any agency's year. One campaign winning five golds is almost unheard of.

In the end, the campaign was hugely successful because Toyota and Saatchi knew that outback blokes had never stopped loving the brand—they just needed to be reminded that Toyota still loved them. The "Border Crossing" campaign did just that, and at the same time, it reminded them that Toyota made the toughest, most reliable, potentially life-saving 4X4s on the market.

And the creek still has not run dry on this idea. Toyota is in the process of launching a new campaign that lovingly and laughingly celebrates "Land Cruiser Country" and the unique people who live there.

Body Language

09

This chapter features case stories for Visa and Nike. The common ground for these stories is their ability to understand that brands do not always need to explain things specifically, but can communicate by having the right body language. Both brands avoid the hard sell and instead "walk the talk" in a way that is authentic, differentiating, and clearly communicates the brands' benefits.

Visa Goes with the Flow

By 2008, Saatchi & Saatchi and Visa had been working together in Europe for more than a decade, but the client-agency relationship was at a crossroads.

That was because Visa's business was changing fundamentally. Advances in digital information technology meant that Visa Europe—a joint venture of 3,400 banks across 32 European countries—was evolving from a straightforward credit-based payment platform into a technology and innovation company. Advances like tapping or waving your card over a reader, or just using your mobile phone to make payments, which are almost second nature to many consumers now, were just starting to be rolled out in the late 2000s.

As technology and customer behaviors changed simultaneously, growth for Visa became focused on making everyday purchases easier and more seamless, with a new emphasis on debit cards and smaller Euro amounts. Therefore, a key communications goal was to convince people that Visa was the best way to pay for little things too. The marketing team would be judged not just on the total number of cards issued, but on the total number of transactions and the average amount spent on each card.

Visa's competitors were starting to change too. Digital players like PayPal and Google were now becoming just as important as old nemeses like Mastercard and American Express. Visa needed to find new solutions to this evolving scenario. They needed more marketing consistency and increased levels of customer engagement. Their messages had been fragmented. Visa was looking for a single, powerful idea that would lead to a consistent campaign for years to come (as their competitor Mastercard had with their "Priceless" campaign). It was so important to Visa that they had already decided to achieve it, with or without Saatchi & Saatchi.

Visa Europe's chief marketing officer, Mariano Dima, and Saatchi & Saatchi Europe's CEO, Robert Senior, took the opportunity to forge a partnership that would both solve the business problem and rekindle the client-agency relationship. They began by co-chairing meetings with the key players from both the client and the agency. Their first job was to define the unique benefit that Visa's superior technology brought to consumers in this new age.

That idea became the campaign theme,

"Life flows better with Visa."

....

"Flow"

Like most great ideas, the solution for Visa was a series of iterations. It started with a positioning statement: "Visa is better money for a better way of life." According to Dima, "We interviewed consumers, retailers, and members. They had a clear and simple focus: our money was quicker and more secure, making their lives better. This was our brand's essence." The positioning was then linked to a clear benefit statement: "Visa helps simplify your life."

Defining the benefit was only half the battle. Great advertising finds a way to articulate the benefit and execute it in a way that is truly unforgettable.

In one of the client-agency team meetings, the group kept trying to find a more compelling way to define the benefit, when the creative director said, "Isn't it all about flow?" Dima and Senior said in unison, "That's it!" They knew instinctively it was a great organizing idea: an idea that works as a linchpin for a variety of integrated marketing communications.

"Flow" really captured what Visa was trying to say. It also helped avoid the common marketing tendency (some would say disease) of becoming overly self-important and self-indulgent. The people working on any product think about it 24 hours a day. They sometimes lose perspective, and become unable to see clearly how the product fits into people's day-to-day lives. Consumers don't think a lot about their credit or debit cards. It is not a pillar of their life. In fact, people usually think about them only when something goes wrong with a transaction. They are, however, enablers. "Life Flows Better with Visa" made it clear that Visa knew it was not the most important thing in people's lives, but did its bit to make every day a little smoother. Visa made your life flow better because it was faster, accepted in more places, and highly secure.

Flow was potentially a big idea, yet it needed to be executed with simplicity, so people would get what it was about without too much explanation. It also needed to be executed with wit and charm, so the advertising, like the line, would avoid self-indulgence. The campaign's first execution appeared in 2008 on television. It would run in 30 languages across Europe. Oh, and it featured a naked man!

"Running Man"
turns a few heads

The naked man ad was a provocative idea. When it was presented internally at Saatchi & Saatchi, along with a number of other ideas, Senior remembered, "We almost started talking ourselves out of it." When he asked Saatchi London's executive creative director, Kate Stanners, which ad she wanted to recommend, she showed no hesitation. She felt the executional idea hit the "spiritual brief." Unlike a strategic brief or creative strategy, which represent flows of logic, she felt this idea captured the gestalt of the brand and what it was trying to say about Visa and its products.

"Running (Naked) Man"

The spot began with a man—naked save for a pair of socks on his feet and holding a Visa debit card in his hand—running in the desert. As he runs out of the desert into rural towns, he passes shops where he is able to get, in succession, some fast food, a pair of overalls to cover himself, and a map. As he gets nearer the city, he is able to get a scooter. Once in the city, he gets a shave, a new suit, and a ring in a jewelry shop. All the while, he never stops running.

He then runs up the steps of a beautiful church and down the aisle, where his bride is waiting. As he goes down the aisle, he shoots a look at his friends, who are smirking. It is now obvious that they left him in the desert naked as part of a bachelor party prank. In the end, the newlyweds are together in an idyllic shot and all is well with the world thanks to Visa's debit card.

The product was at the center of the story, enabling the hero to achieve everything he wanted to do. Stanners noted that the naked man idea was "the best possible demonstration of not needing anything but your Visa card to get your life going."

"Running Man" was an instant hit. The research results for the ad were outstanding. It was a terrific kick-off to a series of memorable ads that are still running to this day, which all share a common executional platform. They are all lighthearted, purposeful journeys that help explain how Visa improves the flow of your daily life.

Bill Shannon
shows off his
unique moves
on crutches

The next journey happened in 2009. The idea had its roots in the Saatchi & Saatchi New Directors' Showcase, which is a yearly staple at the Cannes Lions Festival. The Directors' Showcase is a popular attraction that is very useful to agency creatives and producers looking for new talent. It is the second-most attended event at Cannes each year, next to the festival itself. One of the most interesting films in the showcase that year was a music video for hip-hop producer and musician RJD2 featuring interpretive dance artist Bill Shannon. Shannon, known affectionately as "CrutchMaster" in dance circles, was born with a degenerative hip condition yet he performs highly choreographed dance maneuvers on his specially made crutches. The result is mesmerizing. His movements glide effortlessly and are a joy to watch. There is not a hint of disability, but rather a feeling that his crutches enable him to do amazing things others cannot do.

It did not take long for Saatchi to connect these smooth-flowing movements and Visa's next journey. In the commercial that resulted, viewers saw Shannon's incredible dexterity as he glided down steps and a bannister, into shops and through crowded city streets with his feet never seeming to touch the ground. To the newly initiated, watching the commercial was akin to seeing Michael Jackson's first "moonwalk." As in the "Running Man" ad, Shannon's trip was purposeful. Along his way, he bought a hat, a jacket, and finally a skateboard. Watching him coast through the crowd at the end of the commercial with skateboard and crutches in balletic synchronization provided the commercial's climax, and a perfect canvas for the "Life Flows Better with Visa" tag line. This ad, perhaps more than any other, made clear that Visa "removes obstacles" along the way, every day.

From couch potato to road runner; and
from road runner to World Cup champion

The job for 2010 was a little different. The team needed to develop a new journey consistent with the campaign, but also needed to announce Visa's sponsorship of the 2010 World Cup. In doing so, the 2010 commercial would communicate not only that your life flowed better, but that your life could also get better.

The commercial started with an overweight couch potato watching a football match. He gets so excited when his team scores that he jumps up, grabs his Visa card and starts running. He runs through England, through Europe, through Sub-Saharan Africa and all the way down to South Africa, where the 2010 World Cup is taking place. As in other commercials, he is buying what he needs along the way without breaking stride. In a twist, as he keeps running, he gets thinner and fitter. He gets so fit in fact, that he runs into the World Cup stadium, on to the field and scores a winning goal. He assumes the same celebration dance he did in the beginning, but this time as a champion. The commercial ends with the now familiar "Life Flows Better with Visa" line.

On a humorous inside note, although there was more than one actor used to differentiate the beginning (couch potato) from the end (soccer star), the first actor did so much running during production and rehearsals that he was actually losing weight too fast for some of his scenes.

The TV commercial was part of a fully integrated campaign including cinema, television, online consumer promotions (where, among other things, people could win actual tickets to the World Cup), and other online engagement initiatives.

2012 London Olympics

The World Cup campaign would be a warm-up for Visa's biggest promotional campaign opportunity: the 2012 Summer Olympics in London. As a major Olympic sponsor, and with the Olympics being hosted in Europe, Visa was expected to do something special.

By 2012, consumers' acceptance of both contact-less and mobile payments was gaining traction, and Visa's delivery of both products was excellent. This meant that the speed of transactions had never been faster. In fact, many transactions could be done in as little as half of a second. The strategic goal for Visa and Saatchi for 2012 was to use the Olympics to underscore both "flow" and "speed."

Flow better = flow faster

Speed and the Summer Olympics were a natural fit. So, Visa thought,

"What better way to extend the running man idea than by associating the brand with the fastest man in the world: Jamaican sprinter Usain Bolt?"

The commercial for the Olympics featured Bolt arriving at the airport. His luggage is lost. He eyes another man at the airport, whose luggage is also lost, and the two inexplicably race from the airport all the way through London.

The two use their Visa cards to get around and to get things they need. (Here we see the first overt use of the Visa cellphone application to make a payment.) In Bolt's case, he buys a running outfit. In the other man's case, he buys a green jacket. Bolt runs into the stadium; the other man gets there by boat. Then we realize why they are racing each other. As Bolt sets up in the starting blocks for his race, we see that the other man is the starter, who holds up his pistol to start the race.

The story behind the commercial is as entertaining as the commercial itself. The agency team had a total of 16 hours with Usain Bolt. In that time—which is the typical duration of one commercial shooting day—they needed to get all of their film footage and interviews for TV, print, point-of-sale, PR, digital applications, and even messages to bank CEOs. The team planned their time with Bolt down to 30-second increments.

Bolt insisted on doing his own stunts, like jumping over a luggage cart. Every time he did, the production team's collective hearts were in their mouths. At one point, he began to run on a treadmill in front of a green screen, so the background could be superimposed later. After a few seconds of running, he stopped and started to grab his leg, seemingly in pain. Everybody froze. Had they just hurt the world's fastest man? Had their big idea turned into a disaster? Had they just ruined the Olympics for the whole world? After a few more seconds, they realized he had just tripped. He smiled and said he was fine. The shooting commenced. Whew!

♥

The campaign was a huge success. Usain Bolt became one of the greatest performers and personalities at the Summer Games. Among his other achievements, he set a new Olympic record for the 100 meter run to go with his existing world record, reinforcing his claim as "World's Fastest Man." He was also by far the most flamboyant athlete at the games. He was never too shy to mug in front of the camera, do a little dance, or praise his own performance.

The association with Bolt made a lot of sense, but there was risk involved. He was not British or even European. Before the Olympics, only true athletics fans knew who he was. The average person on the street might not know him at all, and would only get the full impact of the campaign if he did something spectacular at the Games. He did, and the rest is history.

Mariano Dima summarized the campaign as,

"A fun and impactful way to drive customer engagement with the brand."

He believes it "showed how Visa can help people overcome barriers and get one step closer to making their dreams a reality, whatever they may be." He also noted that even calling it a "campaign" is probably a mistake: "It is not a campaign, it is the brand itself. 'Life Flows Better' is not just about communications, it informs our product development. It focuses us on doing things to simplify our consumers' lives, not just develop something for technology's sake." Like the Ritz-Carlton case we saw earlier in the book, the advertising idea has become an operational strategy. "It is the cornerstone of our business," according to Dima.

A shot from the television commercial featuring Brazil vs. Brazil

Fans Re-engaged

Re-engage them it did. In just five days, Nike had over 47,000 mobile interactions with football-obsessed teens. Within 15 days, Nike increased its Facebook fan base by 15% with the Brazilian team as the key topic. The jersey launch commercial, after only a week, became the most watched video in the history of Nike Football Brazil's channel, and took Nike's Brand Channel to first place among brands in Brazil. After just two weeks, it had 4.6 million views and was among the most watched videos in Nike's global history.

The cherry on top was that Brazilian fans and Brazilian players had rediscovered their love for each other. They were connected on the road to 2014 and working together to get Brazil's sixth World Cup title.

Let's not forget that the business goal of the campaign was to launch and sell a new shirt. Shirt sales jumped significantly versus the previous year. Guilherme Glezer, head of brand connections at Nike, attributed success to "total consumer engagement on digital platforms, an epic video, and an intelligent media buy," which delivered "one of the greatest experiences in Brazilian advertising in the last few years."

At its best, Lovemarks thinking helps companies sell products, while touching the hearts of the people it sells them to. Nike's new shirt campaign is a perfect example. Brazil's national shirt now has a chance to be a Lovemark for a whole new generation.

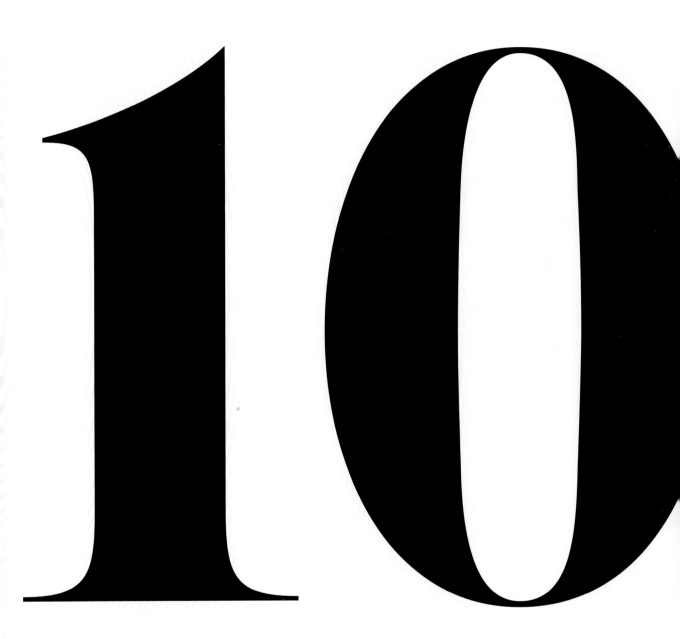

Teasing the Senses

10

This chapter features case stories for *Trident* and BGH. The common ground for these stories is their ability to create brand and product positioning based on sensual appeals. *Trident* does it by figuratively translating the sensual mouth appeal of chewing gum into sensual life appeal and fun. BGH does it by taking products that appeal to one set of senses, and enticing us by appealing to new and surprising ones. Lovemarks and sensuality go hand and hand.

LOVE

TRIDENT CASE STORY

Trident Liberates Their Brand

One of Saatchi & Saatchi's newest global clients is the *Trident* chewing gum brand. *Trident* is part of newly formed global snacks company Mondelēz International (previously Kraft Foods, Inc.). Together, Saatchi & Saatchi and Mondelēz International are developing *Trident* campaigns for North America, South America, Western Europe, the Baltic States, Russia, and the Middle East.

Trident is a landmark product. It was the first sugar free gum to be sold nationally in the United States, and today it is the world's biggest chewing gum brand. It was also the first gum in space, enjoyed by astronauts on the 1964 Gemini space flights. Gum is the fastest-growing confectionary category on earth (last year it grew 4.8% globally), and *Trident* has more than doubled in size since 2003.

With a market position like that, in a growing category, what could be wrong? A lot actually.

To understand *Trident's* challenges, we need to go back to the early 1960s. It was then that the sugarless version of *Trident* was launched behind one of the most famous advertising lines in American history:

"4 out of 5 dentists surveyed recommend sugarless gum for their patients who chew gum."

The campaign was launched by *Trident's* then parent company American Chicle Company (makers of Chiclets) as a response to medical discoveries that linked sugar with dental cavities.

For decades *Trident* would be positioned as a brand that promoted good oral healthcare. Oral care would be a recipe for success for *Trident*. But as we saw with the Safeguard case earlier in this book, functional benefits can only go so far for so long. Over the years, a combination of events would erode the strength of the brand and make its promise less competitive.

One of *Trident*'s classic "4 out of 5 dentists" ad

One event was the explosion of sugar free competitors. *Trident* had the most memorable name in the category, and they were still identified with helping keep cavities at bay, but in reality every sugar free gum could claim the same. Another more recent event was the introduction of a slew of competitive sugar free gums that would bring newfound excitement to the category. They did not talk about oral health; they figured everyone knew that instinctively by now. Brands such as 5 Gum, Stride, and Orbit came out with quirky, fun advertising campaigns, new flavors, and innovative, colorful packaging.

In the midst of this evolved, redefined category, *Trident* was still the biggest name, but no longer the closest to the consumer's heart. Jason Levine, vice president of marketing for global gum and candy for Mondelēz International, put it succinctly: "We were respected, but not loved." The brand was losing its saliency and relevance amongst younger consumers. So the *Trident* business went up for competitive agency pitch in mid-2011, and it aligned itself with the Lovemarks agency. According to Levine,

"**At Mondelēz International we talk about powerful brands connecting to people with fundamental human truths in an emotional way. Saatchi talks about Lovemarks. It's the same thing. Trident should be a Lovemark, and we are working together to make it one.**"

It's All about the Fun

Saatchi & Saatchi's New York office was leading the pitch and working with Saatchi offices worldwide. As we have seen so many times in this book, they started by conducting an Xploring exercise. "We deployed Saatchi planners in key markets, including US, Argentina, Brazil, Mexico, Spain, and France," said Saatchi's global account director Nick Miaritis. "We also conducted what we called 'Self-Xploration.' We asked consumers to record their self-reflections when and where they were thinking of chewing gum. We even gave them cameras. From this, we were able to extract insights from individual ethnographies."

What they learned was simple but important. Unlike previous generations, *Trident's* core audience of Millennials (defined by *Trident* as 18–35 year olds) do not see fun as something that should happen occasionally. They see it as something that should be baked into everything they do. This was a very different sensibility from baby boomers for example, who grew up with *Trident*. In Miaritis's words,

"Fun shouldn't be relegated to Happy Hour on Thursday night."

Worryingly, the research also showed that fun was at an all-time low for Millennials. The world around us is increasingly variable, complex, and uncertain, with unemployment among young people at very high levels in many countries. The *Trident* team concluded, therefore, that fun is under siege worldwide, and that gum was an antidote.

These findings reinforced the feelings the *Trident* brand team had about their product. When they asked people about why they purchased gum, they got lots of perfunctory functional responses, like the need to "freshen my breath," or the desire for "minty taste." *Trident* calls these "mouth occasions." But when they asked people how it made them feel, the responses were exciting and emotional, like "It makes me feel happy," "It de-stresses me," "It makes me like myself better." *Trident* calls these "mood occasions." It was clear to the team that focusing on mood occasions could be a huge opportunity.

A precedent for equating *Trident* with fun came from South America. Brazil is *Trident's* second-largest global market. *Trident* in Brazil had already been focusing on fun for quite some time with a tremendous amount of success. (But then who knows more about fun than Brazilians?) Therefore, one of the key goals for the team was to capture the spirit *Trident* had in Brazil and spread it everywhere.

By 2011 things were not all bad for *Trident*. The brand was riding a wave of innovation. They had introduced many *Trident* variants, including *Trident* White (for tooth whitening), *Trident* Extra Care, *Trident* Splash, and *Trident* Layers. The problem was that its heritage with consumers was about oral care, which was not necessarily where they wanted to be any longer. Their new products were split between oral care (e.g. *Trident* White and *Trident* Extra Care) and fun/flavorful (e.g. *Trident* Splash and *Trident* Layers). "*Trident* had a split personality. People didn't know what we stood for," was Jason Levine's assessment.

The advertising objectives for Saatchi and *Trident* were two-fold. First, make *Trident* fun. The focus would need to be on enjoyment versus protection. Second, unify the brand and all of its diverse variants under one brand image, one brand promise, regardless of specific product function. The team referred to this as "unleashing the power of one *Trident*."

The strategic idea that Saatchi and the *Trident* brand team developed was as simple as the consumer insight itself:

"*Trident* Liberates Fun"

"Liberation" was the key to the creative solution. In a world where fun is hard to come by, you can unlock it yourself, and let it loose, by doing something as simple as popping a piece of *Trident*. This was also a deliberate aspect to *Trident's* Lovemarks strategy. It focused on the sensuality of the gum chewing-experience, where all of the emotions and pleasure are.

See What Unfolds

Liberating fun eventually turned into the advertising campaign line "See What Unfolds." In other words, once you pop a piece of *Trident*, it is like a smile for your brain that starts in your mouth, which puts you in the right frame of mind for fun. When you feel that way, anything can happen, and it's almost always good. *Trident* has used this campaign idea as a license to spread fun across the airwaves, the web, point of sale, radio, and print media.

A key reason why Saatchi was awarded the business was because of its strong creative talent in markets around the world, especially key markets like the US, Brazil, Argentina, Russia, and the UK. These offices would be charged with finding ways to liberate fun and execute "See What Unfolds" in locally relevant ways.

To get an idea of just how global the creative process would become, the client and agency teams travelled to Istanbul (where East meets West) to review creative advertising ideas from Saatchi offices worldwide.

When the advertising ideas were put into concept form, they were tested using both qualitative and quantitative techniques from top research companies like Millward Brown. The results were very strong. *Trident* was now ready to launch their first global campaign.

Some of the campaign's most interesting ideas have been about taking things that are tedious or dull and liberating them with *Trident*. For example, in April 2012, during the height of the US tax return season, *Trident* launched an online video that transformed a tax audit (what is more unfun than tax returns?) into a "fun audit" by tapping into your Facebook page—with your prior approval of course. It went through your pictures, messages, and links, integrating them into the online video with hilarious effect, and giving you a score for how much fun is happening in your life.

The algorithm that drove the video had over 200 personalized responses and 300 key words. So for example, if your Facebook page had a picture of you and your friends in Las Vegas, the audit would show the picture and produce a tailored message like, "What happens in Vegas stays in Vegas." At the end, the video increased your fun by providing a coupon for *Trident* and a flavor recommendation based on your unique profile.

The "Fun Audit" campaign got a big awareness boost when TV star Jimmy Kimmel featured it on his popular late-night show (he received a fun score of 73%).

Trident's Online "Fun Audit"

In Colombia, *Trident* ran a Twitter-based campaign where people could tweet their ideas for making the world a more fun place. They took the best ones and made them a reality. Someone asked, "What if we could make traffic jams more fun?" So *Trident* set up karaoke machines in areas with bad traffic. Someone asked "Why don't we break open piñatas every day instead of just birthdays?" *Trident* did. Someone asked, "Why don't we change the names of Colombian towns like El Aburrido (which translates to "boring") and El Llanto (which translates to "crying")?" *Trident* got millions of Colombians to vote to change El Aburrido's name to El Alegre (which translates to "cheerful). In Brazil, a commercial for the campaign shows that anything can happen in a pet store. When a young man pops a piece of *Trident*, the fish, iguanas, and even the little decorative Japanese cats break into a choral rendition of Queen's "Bohemian Rhapsody." It's impossible to watch the commercial without smiling.

Liberating Your Fun in Person

Levine's personal favorites are when *Trident* allows people to experience the brand and liberate fun in person. For example, in June 2012, on an average Wednesday night, *Trident* took over New York's trendiest music spot, Terminal 5, a tri-level venue that is home to the hottest music stars, DJs, and indie bands. Electronic dance music (EDM) is the fastest growing music genre of all time. So *Trident* teamed up with Steve Aoki, electro house musician, record producer, and Dim Mak Records founder. As a surprise, the popular international 80s band Duran Duran appeared along with Aoki. They performed a remix of their signature tune "Hungry Like the Wolf." The place was mobbed with fans of both acts, spanning all ages.

The mix of the two artists created a really interesting blend. *Advertising Age* magazine also noted the unusual chemistry: "On a sweltering night in New York, three unlikely things merged: electronica god Steve Aoki, Duran Duran, and *Trident* gum." When they did, it was clear to everyone:

"See What Unfolds" was more than just a slogan.

"See What Unfolds Live" concert

Beyond the personal experiences, which were of course limited to the number of people who could jam the venue, the Aoki/Duran Duran concert attracted 1.3 million YouTube views and over 345 million PR impressions. It received over 14 million impressions on Facebook and over one million on Twitter.

The "Hungry Like the Wolf" remix was downloaded over 30,000 times. Some of the downloads were done right at the concert because *Trident* handed out special packs of gum with codes to download the track for free.

In 2013 *Trident* plans to take "See What Unfolds Live" on the road. But the concerts are just one example of many experiences *Trident* is staging worldwide. In London, they set up a *Trident* "See What Unfolds" vending machine. Every time someone pressed the button, a musician or street performer would come out of the machine, hand the person some gum, and start performing. By the end, there was an entire troupe of musicians and performers entertaining what had now become a crowd. As with the T-Mobile campaign earlier in this book, the idea has even more power when people experience it in person.

Early Days Are Good Days

These are early days for the campaign. Saatchi and *Trident* have only been working together for about a year, and the campaign has only been in-market for about four months. The results so far, however, are very promising. In the US, *Trident* has had four months of solid share growth reversing a decline, and consumers are feeding back that the brand is more "modern," more "fun," and "a brand I can relate to."

And the people working on *Trident* are having fun too. In the process of presenting the campaign, the team was in Moscow. At a critical juncture of the presentation, they were told in a grave tone that "there is no word for fun in Russian." They thought they were sunk. When it was explained that there is just no single word for fun—different kinds of fun are expressed differently—they burst out laughing. With the right translation, the Russians too were ready to liberate fun.

BGH CASE STORY

BGH's Sound Strategy

As *Trident* has used the sensuality of the chewing gum experience to unleash fun, BGH has been engaging all of the senses to position their appliances as more fun and interesting than the average air conditioner or microwave oven.

BGH is Argentina's top home appliance brand. In collaboration with their agency Del Campo Saatchi & Saatchi, they have a long track record of doing creative, engaging advertising campaigns. For example, one campaign for BGH's air conditioners—which provide five stages of filtered air—featured a giant nose in Argentina's key retail stores. People put their heads inside the "Nose-O-Meter." If their nose was big enough to push the button deep inside, an alarm went off and they received a 25% discount on the air conditioner. Who needs fresh air more than people with large noses? The campaign's theme was

"Pure air for those who need it most."

According to Flora Proverbio, Saatchi's head of planning in Argentina, "With 'Big Nose' we wanted to create a more intimate conversation with consumers, staying away from technical speak, which is cold, distant, and more than anything, pretty generic in this category." The agency's CEO, Pablo Del Campo, had a similar outlook:

"BGH knows that to stand out in this category in Argentina, the brand needs to break conventions. This campaign starts from a wonderful place, almost unique, and is brave enough to not be afraid to look ridiculous. In fact, it embraces it."

"Big Nose"

One of Saatchi's most recent ideas, for BGH's microwave ovens, showed their appreciation for sensuality in building Lovemark brands. As a companion piece to the Swiffer "Touch" case story that appeared in chapter one, this is a fitting case story for the end of this book because the campaign was built on sensory gratification: on sound.

BGH was the share-of-mind leader in the category, but it was seen as a brand for older consumers. It had lower marks than international competitors, like Whirlpool and Samsung, for such things as product design, innovation, and youthfulness.

The breakthrough idea for BGH microwaves came at four o'clock in the morning at Saatchi's offices, as the agency team was working deep into the night. One of the agency creative people was reheating a cup of coffee in the microwave when the loud, shrill, annoying "beep, beep, beep" went off to announce that the coffee was done. Then it struck them. No one likes that beeping noise, especially at four in the morning! They thought,

Discounts for people with big noses!

"What if microwave ovens could be pleasing instead of annoying when they are done with their work? What if they could be downright fun?"

Their solution was simple: replace the beeper with your favorite song. The agency was not recommending a new campaign; they were recommending a redesign of the product. BGH saw the beauty of the idea and after six months of product testing and working side-by-side with the agency in a true environment of co-creation, they had invented a microwave that would allow users to program their favorite tunes.

The product was unprecedented in the history of microwave ovens. The BGH "Quick Chef Music" microwave was equipped with a USB port and speakers. The team was thrilled when they witnessed the first test of the product and heard the microwave announce the food was ready accompanied by Guns N' Roses' rousing "Sweet Child of Mine."

The product was launched with a limited edition of 1,000 microwaves. BGH sold out of stock in just one week. The greatest appeal was to the young consumers the brand coveted, and the brand's scores for product design, innovation, and youthfulness all rose.

The campaign engaged a younger audience on the web and went viral. At www.bghmusic.com, people could sing and record their own recipes. The site became a repository of hundreds of sung microwave-food recipes that people could share socially and download to listen to on their microwaves.

Why did the music-microwave campaign work so well? Because music is very closely related to our sense of identity. A study conducted by Adrian North at Heriot-Watt University in Edinburgh showed that musical preferences and personalities are very closely associated. Another study by Rentfrow and Gosling at the University of Texas revealed that people believe music does more to show who we really are than the movies we watch, the books we read, or even the clothes we wear.

The first microwave that plays music when your food is ready

Saatchi and BGH made microwaves a product that appealed to all of the senses. The senses of sight, touch, and especially smell and taste, had always been there. Now people could appreciate the sound of food. Music soothes the savage breast, and in this case the savage microwave.

BGH's marketing director, Ezequiel Devoto, believes that powerful sensory insights like the music-microwave have helped bring the brand closer to people. He amusingly compares it to being attracted to someone new: "It's like wanting to meet a girl, and after you make a clever remark, she rewards you with a smile." The agency and client celebrated the success of the idea with a dinner at the Del Campo Saatchi & Saatchi offices. Of course, dinner was prepared using the BGH Quick Chef Music Microwave Oven.

Campaigns like "Big Nose" and "Music Microwave" are key reasons why BGH manages to lead the category in recall, top-of-mind awareness, and sales, despite competing against global brands with larger advertising budgets.

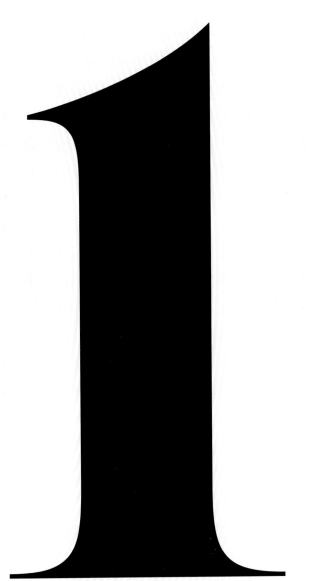

Blood Relations

This book has featured a number of famous brands that have made strong emotional connections with their consumers with the help of Saatchi & Saatchi. This chapter features a project where Saatchi & Saatchi made their own emotional connection to help solve one of the world's most difficult briefs.

Saatchi & Saatchi Gives Blood

Siham Abu Awwad is a Palestinian woman. She describes her heartbreak at losing her 32-year-old brother, Yussef, who was killed by the Israeli Defense Forces (IDF) during the Intifada. She says her overriding emotion at the time was to get revenge.

Ben Kfir is an Israeli man. He describes losing his daughter, Yael, to a Palestinian suicide bomber at the tender age of 21. His overriding emotion was also revenge. In fact, he had even formulated a specific plan to take his two revolvers, go to a nearby construction site with Palestinian laborers, and start shooting.

Both Ben and Siham had premonitions about their loved ones being dead even before being told. They could just feel it. Both felt empty and angry for a long time.

These stories are not uncommon in the Israeli–Palestinian conflict, which has been raging for more than half a century. What is different in this case, however, is that Ben and Siham rose above their common anger and desire for revenge. They embraced their common sense of loss and helped form the Parents Circle Families Forum. The Forum is a grassroots non-profit organization that brings together bereaved families from both sides of the conflict. Their long-term vision is to create a constructive dialogue as a means to build a framework for a reconciliation process.

How this group, Saatchi & Saatchi, a French creative director, and former Israeli Prime Minister Shimon Peres came together for positive change is the story of a great creative challenge set out by BBR Saatchi & Saatchi Tel Aviv. That challenge was laid out to the entire advertising industry and led to a surprising and highly symbolic idea.

Israeli and Palestinian members of the Parents Circle Families Forum embrace

The Impossible Brief

Every project at every Saatchi & Saatchi office in the world starts with a brief. The brief outlines the creative challenge that needs to be solved. The Saatchi team in Tel Aviv decided to see if the same process that was used to solve some of the world's more tenacious marketing problems could be used to help solve the Israeli–Palestinian conflict. They called it the "impossible brief" because they knew that some of the greatest minds in the world had tried and failed: politicians, renowned celebrities, world leaders, even Nobel Prize winners. The group at Saatchi was not so naive as to believe that one creative idea would just solve this intractable conflict; but they knew the power of creativity to influence people's emotions for the better—they had seen it in action their whole careers. They believed deeply that a great idea could only make the future brighter.

For a brief this big, the team knew instinctively that they needed to open it up beyond the agency to the best creative minds worldwide. So they launched the brief at the 2010 Cannes Lions Festival as a challenge to the whole advertising industry.

Here is what the brief said:

Background
The Israeli–Palestinian conflict has been going on for over 60 years. To date, political leaders have failed in reaching a diplomatic solution to create a sense of closeness between the two nations.

The Objective
Rather than "out of date" policies, we need "out of the box" solutions. Let's show the world that creative minds at their best can inspire even political leaders.

The Task
Send us your original, creative, and truly inspiring suggestions for how to bring Israelis and Palestinians closer together.

The Result
The most inspiring solutions will be judged in partnership with The Peres Centre for Peace by Palestinian, Israeli, and international judges. The winner will receive a ticket to the 2011 Cannes Lions, and who knows, you may win a Nobel Peace Prize.

The balanced judging panel was important. According to Yossi Lubaton, CEO of BBR Saatchi & Saatchi, "This was a joint Palestinian–Israeli project from the beginning. There was no patronizing or cynicism on either side, just a group of people who wanted to present the conflict in a more optimistic way." Until now, optimism was something that had been in very short supply. Lubaton noted that people in the Middle East, and worldwide, are always exposed to the conflict in political terms, where the emphasis is on cynicism, argument, counter-argument, and occasionally extreme violence.

This was a chance to show the conflict on another level, a balanced approach with a view to underline the real, ever-present elements of hope. Starting from optimism was, in itself, a potential breakthrough.

Blood Relations

BBR Saatchi & Saatchi received scores of proposals. The finalist ideas were composed in a book and sent to political leaders around the world under the auspices of Shimon Peres' Centre for Peace.

The winning idea was devastatingly simple. It came from Jean-Christophe Royar, an award-winning creative director at the BETC agency in Paris. It was called,

"Mutual Blood"

The idea was based on the premise that despite our strong differences, we are all brothers and sisters in blood. Our common blood underscores our shared humanity.

Could you hurt someone who has your blood running through their veins?

Royar recommended creating the Israeli–Palestinian Blood Donation Project, a high-profile blood drive for all peace-loving Israelis and Palestinians. They would donate their blood together for the needs of each other's communities. The idea was underscored by a challenging thought: "Could you hurt someone who has your blood running through their veins?" Beyond the basic need for blood, the donation project had highly symbolic meaning in a conflict where far too much blood has been spilled over the years, on both sides.

"'Mutual Blood' was selected by the judges as the leading example of the fearless creativity that defines our industry," according to Lubaton. Dr. Aliza Savir, deputy director general of The Peres Centre, added that, "Because of the prolonged conflict afflicting the region, we are unfortunately witnessing an accelerated process of dehumanization, and there is an urgent need to stress the human dimension of this conflict. This campaign conveys two messages: first, the fact that we are all humans and have the same blood, and second, the fact that we all basically aspire to the same thing, which is simply to live."

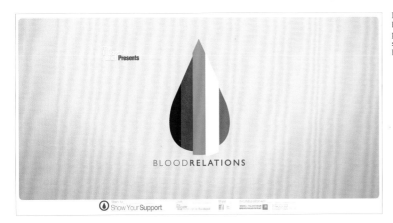

In addition to actual blood donations, people could show their support by donating blood virtually, online

BLOOD**RELATIONS**

Saatchi approached the Parents Circle Families Forum to help rally support on both sides of the political and cultural fence. They were the key to making the idea happen. Siham Abu Awwad and Ben Kfir, mentioned earlier, also appeared in an eight-minute internet film telling their stories and showing them with other bereaved Palestinians and Israelis, giving blood side by side. As Awwad stated in the film,

"Maybe the language of blood is stronger than anything else."

....

The campaign's timing leveraged the flashpoint of the United Nations vote on Palestinian Statehood on September 14, 2011. The film itself was premiered by Saatchi at The Peres Centre during a special event marking the UN International Day of Peace on September 21, 2011.

Beyond live donations at the Israeli Blood Bank and an Islamic hospital that agreed to accept blood from both sides, mobile blood donation trucks were set up in places like Tel Aviv's Cinematheque Square. In addition, a website and Facebook page were set up so people worldwide could donate blood, virtually, to support the project. Israeli supermodel, Bar Refaeli, was one of the first to tweet her support, and urged her 60,000 Twitter followers to do the same.

Live donations also took off beyond the Middle East. In November 2011, in cities worldwide, Arabs and Israelis gave blood together. In London, for example, Jewish, Muslim, and international students flocked to blood centers. Israel's ambassador to England, H.E. Daniel Taub, who participated in the blood drive, stated:

"As a combat medic in the IDF, I learned that issues of life and death can help bridge the divide. I am very moved to see people reaching out to each other in such an important and creative way."

....

Seeing is believing

The campaign's goal was as simple as the idea: to reach as many people as possible in Israel and beyond. Seeing the video of perceived sworn enemies giving blood side by side was enough to change prejudices, communicate optimism, and inspire hope for better days in the future.

Despite a tiny budget, the idea's simplicity and raw imagery led to an avalanche of free publicity. National news in Israel picked up the story, generating a 24 rating (i.e., 24% of all Israelis saw it). Internationally, it was picked up by the likes of NBC, BBC, and Reuters. Hundreds of blogs, news publications, and radio stations did likewise. In the end, 350 million people worldwide knew about it. Hillary Clinton picked up on it and gave it the backing of the US State Department, presenting it to the heads of key UN missions.

Israelis and Palestinians giving blood side by side

Former Prime Minister
Shimon Peres and
Saatchi & Saatchi
CEO Worldwide
Kevin Roberts

BBR Saatchi & Saatchi received the prestigious United Nations Gold Award. It was the first time an Israeli agency had been so awarded. Unsurprisingly, Saatchi & Saatchi's Worldwide Creative Board named it the Idea of the Year for the global network.

Yossi Lubaton related it to Saatchi & Saatchi's global mission:

"The motto we live by in all our work is that nothing is impossible. And surely the fact that, even during such a politically sensitive time, we managed to launch the 'Blood Relations' idea in collaboration with the Parents Circle Families Forum and The Peres Centre for Peace, is the greatest testament to that notion."

Earlier in this book, The Ritz-Carlton showed us that brands can transcend marketing and make a personal impact. BBR Saatchi & Saatchi Tel Aviv's impossible brief reinforces the idea that brands can make a difference. They can transform negative emotions of fear and hate into positive emotions of love and caring.

On a final note, Yossi Lubaton mentioned that everyone who worked on the project, Palestinians and Israelis, become very emotionally involved and ended up in tears when viewing the eight-minute "Blood Relations" film.

This book has featured a number of stories referring to people shedding tears when looking at advertising communications. It has also profiled the extreme feelings of emotion and pride for those working on the ideas.

In the rough and tumble world of advertising, a focus on "Filling the World with Lovemarks" makes days at work fun and fulfilling for thousands of people; and it makes watching the end result inspirational for hundreds of millions of people worldwide.

The campaign was recognized by five gold Lion awards at Cannes in 2012. That is the most awards ever won by an Israeli agency in Cannes history.

Conclusion

Love is working

Chapter one of this book set the stage. It described Lovemarks theory in detail. We learned that brands could foster mystery, sensuality, and intimacy to move from being respected to being loved. We also learned that when brands do this successfully, they have the opportunity to create "loyalty beyond reason," the kind of loyalty that supports premium pricing, resists cross-shopping, and gives the brand the benefit of the doubt should it make a misstep.

Since the publication of *Lovemarks* in 2004, one criticism it has received is that it did not provide an exact road map for becoming a Lovemark. In other words, it did not lay out a precise set steps for brands to follow to become a Lovemark, per se.

Life and marketing are not always that simple.

....

As we have seen in this book, there are many paths to becoming a Lovemark. Different brands in different categories with unique competitors, distinct histories, and different emotional relationships with their consumers took very different journeys. What this book has shown, however, is that if a brand sets its goal on love, and makes the hard decisions to stay the course, it is always rewarded by their customers in the marketplace. We have seen that result over and over again for some of the world's biggest and most successful brands, including Toyota, Procter & Gamble, General Mills, The Ritz-Carlton, Miller, Diageo, Visa, and Nike.

Now for some very good news. For those who are looking for a step-by-step approach, the cases we have seen in this book actually provide one. It is a four-step program:

◆ STEP 1

Discovery

This is the search for the truth about your business, the opportunities and the issues. The emphasis here is on honesty, seeing your business for what it is, not what you want it to be. In Pampers' case for example, they were brutally honest about the trust they had lost due to the DryMax saga.

◆ STEP 2

Exploration

This is the process of getting to the truth about consumers, the revelation and insights. Ethnography can be a great tool here, and we saw a number of great examples of clients using Saatchi's proprietary Xploring technique. For example, Xploring led to the insight that there is a "Drop of Greatness" in every African man, not just in the Bond-esque Michael Power.

◆ STEP 3

Inspiration

Inspiration is what comes out of our most creative strategic thinking; it is the launch pad for great organizing ideas. As we have seen, many of the brands in this book made use of "Tribes" to gain inspiration from the strategy process and get to big ideas. In the case of Cheerios, we saw a group of diverse individuals from inside and outside the client and agency meet in a Minneapolis oat field. Together they discovered that the answer was all about simplicity, which led to the simplest idea of all: single words punctuated by a Cheerio on a yellow background.

♥ STEP 4

Attraction

Attraction is about inspiring consumer participation. It means everyday people own the idea and share it with others. The Camry Effect had it. So did the Reebok Japan exercise video and the Miller High Life one-second commercial. In fact, every single case featured in this book has strong aspects of consumer attraction and involvement. The key to attraction in the digital age is to understand the relationship between brand affection and social media. As I mentioned in the beginning of this book, Lovemarks was years ahead of its time. It is more relevant in the age of digital media than it has ever been. Brand love and brand advocacy are now the same thing.

So, for those of you who wanted a step-by-step roadmap, you've got one. It will only work if you have the guts to stay the course, avoid the temptation to think like a sales organization, and start by loving your consumer first.

The introduction to this book quoted the book review editor at *Advertising Age*. As we end, it is only fitting to quote him again:

♥

....

"Lovemarks screams at you that advertising is a creative enterprise. That what we are engaged in here is not just facts and figures. It is different. It is innovative. It is unusual. That we are trying to get people—on both sides of the transaction—to think about things differently."

....

Martin Bihl

Index

Other Titles

Lovemarks: the future beyond brands

By Kevin Roberts, CEO Worldwide, Saatchi & Saatchi

Foreword by A.G. Lafley

ISBN: 978-1-57687-270-3

Published 2004, powerHouse Books

A business revolution is changing the rules of the marketplace. Power is shifting from manufacturers and retailers directly to consumers, freshly enabled with information, choice, and connectivity. Price, service, quality, and design advantages are no longer enough to win.

In *Lovemarks: the future beyond brands*, Kevin Roberts shows how mystery, sensuality, and intimacy can create powerful emotional connections with consumers and inspire "Loyalty Beyond Reason." Now published in 18 languages, with 250,000 copies in print, *Lovemarks* has won the hearts of business owners, marketing directors, and consumers worldwide. It speaks a new, fresh, common language—the language of love. *Lovemarks* is the book companion to the widely populated website lovemarks.com.

"Ideas move mountains, especially in turbulent times. *Lovemarks* is the product of the fertile iconoclast mind of Kevin Roberts, CEO Worldwide of Saatchi & Saatchi. Roberts argues vociferously, and with a ton of data to support him, that traditional branding practices have become stultified. What's needed are customer Love affairs. Roberts lays out his grand scheme for mystery, magic, sensuality, and the like in his gloriously designed book *Lovemarks*." —Tom Peters

The Lovemarks Effect:
winning in the consumer revolution

By Kevin Roberts, CEO Worldwide,
Saatchi & Saatchi

ISBN: 978-1-57687-267-3

Published 2006, powerHouse Books

In this follow-up book to *Lovemarks: the future beyond brands*, the voices of consumers, owners, and marketers show the impact of Lovemarks on their lives, their businesses, and their aspirations. *The Lovemarks Effect* offers instruction and inspiration about creating emotional connections and winning in a consumer-empowered "attraction economy." How consumers feel about you— their emotional connection to you—is what determines success.

Contributors include marketing maverick Tom Peters, Nobel physicist Arno Penzias, *New Yorker* writer Malcolm Gladwell, designer Mary Quant, Toyota engineer Inoue Masao, and marketers Jim Stengel and John Fleming. CEOs from world-winning brands such as Victorinox, Diesel, Tiffany & Co., Aveda, Montblanc, Benetton, and Lonely Planet share unique stories about the potential of *Lovemarks*, and the power of "Loyalty Beyond Reason."

The Lovemarks Effect also showcases the findings of QiQ International's Lovemarks research in a 12-page feature. The study validates the cornerstone qualities that help to shift a brand to a Lovemark, and finds there is conclusive evidence that creating a Lovemark will increase sales, preference, and usage.

From the aisles of the in-store experience to the power of sustainable enterprise, from Lovemarks research to consumer stories, *The Lovemarks Effect* is a joyride through the evolving business landscape.

Basics:
Online Marketing

By Brian Sheehan, Associate Professor of
Advertising, S.I. Newhouse School of Public
Communications, Syracuse University

ISBN: 978-2940411337

2010, AVA Publishing

....

In a digital world, marketers are running scared. Brands
are having a hard time coping with both the pace of change
and the challenge to their time-tested business models.
To make things worse, there is a dearth of good literature
on the subject. Business people and students of all kinds
are often left in the lurch. Without a basic "how to" guide,
they need to figure things out for themselves, or sadly, just
react to the allure of the new hot thing, often proselytized
by charlatans.

Brian Sheehan teaches Online Marketing at the S.I.
Newhouse School of Public Communications at Syracuse
University. He figured he would help solve the problem
by turning his introductory class into a basic guide for
professionals and students alike.

Basics: Online Marketing breaks down digital marketing
into its most important components: search marketing,
e-commerce, e-branding, online advertising, the social
web, online applications, mobile marketing, measurement
& analytics, and online ethics. The book is a guide to major
online trends that exemplify forward thinking, and which
will continue to inspire online ideas well into the future.

International examples, case studies, and practical
exercises help the reader master the key concepts and
techniques of online marketing so they can apply them
quickly in the real world.

Basics:
Marketing Management

By Brian Sheehan, Associate Professor of
Advertising, S.I. Newhouse School of Public
Communications, Syracuse University

ISBN: 978-2940411511

2011, AVA Publishing SA

....

After 25 years in advertising, and 15 years as CEO of
Saatchi & Saatchi offices from Japan to Australia to
Los Angeles, Brian Sheehan decided to write the book
that he wished he had been given when put in his first
management role.

Basics: Marketing Management is a repository of
invaluable business skills, ideas, and tools for students and
practitioners of marketing. Understanding how to create
marketing programs is one thing. Understanding how to
take leadership in all business areas related to marketing
programs is another thing entirely. It entails facility with
economics, finances, personnel management, and long-
term strategy. Sheehan helps bridge the divide with simple,
practical lessons garnered from years of experience, and
from top business leaders and thinkers.

Specific topics include: Economic principles; vision
and mission statements; competitive business strategy;
brand identity and thought leadership; managing people;
handling a crisis; measurement, analytics, and financial
basics; legal considerations; and ethical issues.

Further Reading

BOOKS

Ariely, Dan. *Predictably Irrational: The Hidden Forces That Shape Our Decisions.* New York: Harper Perennial, 2010.

Damasio, Antonio. *The Feeling of What Happens: Body, Emotion and the Making of Consciousness.* New York: Mariner Books, 2010.

Gardner, Howard. *Changing Minds: The Art and Science of Changing Our Own and Other People's Minds.* Massachusetts: Harvard Business Review Press, 2006.

Gobé, Marc. *Emotional Branding: The New Paradigm for Connecting Brands to People.* New York: Allworth Press, 2010.

Goodson, Scott. *Uprising: How to Build a Brand—and Change the World—By Sparking Cultural Movements.* Ohio: McGraw-Hill, 2012.

Heath, Chip and Dan Heath. *Made to Stick: Why Some Ideas Survive and Others Die.* New York: Random House, 2007.

Hill, Dan. *Emotionomics: Winning Hearts and Minds.* Minnesota: Adams Business & Professional, 2007.

Iezzi, Teressa. *The Idea Writers: Copywriting in a New Media and Marketing Era.* New York: Palgrave Macmillan, 2010.

Kawasaki, Guy. *Enchantment: The Art of Changing Hearts, Minds, and Actions.* New York: Portfolio Hardcover, 2011.

Kim, W. Chan, and Renée Mauborgne. *Blue Ocean Strategy: How to Create Uncontested Market Space and Make Competition Irrelevant.* Massachusetts: Harvard Business Review Press, 2005.

Lecinski, Jim. *Winning the Zero Moment of Truth – ZMOT.* New York: Vook, 2011.

Lindstrom, Martin. *Buyology: Truth and Lies About Why We Buy.* New York: Crown Business, 2010.

Lusensky, Jakob. *Sounds Like Branding: Use the Power of Music to Turn Consumers Into Fans.* London: Bloomsbury Publishing, 2011.

O'Shaughnessy, John, and Nicholas Jackson O'Shaughnessy. *The Marketing Power of Emotion.* New York: Oxford University Press, 2002.

Roberts, Kevin. *Lovemarks: the future beyond brands.* New York: powerHouse Books, 2004.

Roberts, Kevin. *The Lovemarks Effect: winning in the consumer revolution.* New York: powerHouse Books, 2006.

Rose, Frank. *The Art of Immersion: How the Digital Generation is Remaking Hollywood, Madison Avenue, and the Way We Tell Stories.* New York: W. W. Norton & Company, 2012.

Sisodia, Rajendra. S., David B. Wolfe, and Jagdish N. Sheth. *Firms of Endearment: How World-Class Companies Profit from Passion and Purpose.* New Jersey: Pearson Prentice Hall, 2007.

Walker, Rob. *Buying In: The Secret Dialogue Between What We Buy and Who We Are.* New York: Random House, 2008.

Zaltman, Gerald. *How Customers Think: Essential Insights Into the Mind of the Market.* Massachusetts: Harvard Business Review Press, 2003.

Further Reading cont.

PAPERS

Ahuvia, Aaron, and Barbara Carroll. "Some Antecedents and Outcomes of Brand Love." *Marketing Letters* 17.2 (2006): 79–89.

Albert, Noël, Dwight Merunka, and Pierre Valette-Florence. "When Consumers Love Their Brands: Exploring the Concept and its Dimensions." *Journal of Business Research* 61.10 (2007): 1062–1075.

Altman, Kayla, et al. "Love is in the Heart: Physiological Responding to Preferred Brands." University of Mannheim, 2008. Web. 27 Mar 2008.

Baker, Monica, et al. "In Search of Lovemarks: the Semantic Structure of Brands." *Proceedings of the American Academy of Advertising* (2007): 42–29.

Batra, Rajeev, Aaron Ahuvia, and Richard P. Bagozzi. "Brand Love." *Journal of Marketing* 76.2 (2011): 1–16.

Bauer, Hans H., Daniel Heinrich, and Isabel Martin. "How to Create High Emotional Consumer–Brand Relationships? The Causalities–Brand Passion." University of Mannheim, 2007. Web. 14 Nov 2011.

Bergkvist, Lars, and Tino Bech-Larsen. "Two Studies of Consequences and Actionable Antecedents of Brand Love." *Journal of Brand Management* 17 (2010): 504–518.

Cooper, Peter, and John Pawle. "Measuring Emotion — Lovemarks, the Future Beyond Brands." *Journal of Advertising Research* 46.1 (2006): 38-48.

Ewing, Douglas. "When Does Brand Matter? An Empirical Examination of the Roles of Attachment, Experience, and Identity within Consumer–Brand Relationships." Diss. University of Cincinnati, 2010. Web. 17 Jul 2012.

Fournier, Susan. "Consumers and Their Brands: Developing Relationship Theory in Consumer Research." *Journal of Marketing* 24.4 (1998): 343-373.

Govers, Pascalle C.M., and Ruth Mugge. "'I Love My Jeep, Because It's Tough Like Me', The Effect of Product–Personality Congruence on Product Attachment." Diss. Nyenrode University and Delft University of Technology, 2011. Web. 14 Nov 2011.

Heinrich, Daniel, Hans H. Bauer, and Johannes C. M. Mühl. "Measuring Brand Love: Applying Sternberg's Triangular Theory of Love in Consumer–Brand Relations." University of Mannheim, 2008. Web. 10 Oct 2008.

Kim, Hye-Young, Youn-Kyung Kim, Laura Jolly, and Ann Fairhurst. "Satisfied Customers' i.e. Love toward Retailers: A Cross-Product Exploration." *Advances in Consumer Research* 35 (2008): 507–515.

Lerner, Jennifer S., Deborah A. Small, and George Loewenstein. "Heart Strings and Purse Strings." *Psychological Science* 15.5 (2004): 337–341.

Lundqvist, Anna, et al. "The Impact of Storytelling on the Consumer Brand Experience: The Case of a Firm-Originated Story." *Journal of Brand Management* (2012). Web. 2 Mar/2012.

MacInnis, Deborah J., C. Whan Park, and Matthew Thomson. "The Ties That Bind: Measuring the Strength of Consumers' Emotional Attachments to Brands." *Journal of Consumer Psychology* 15.1 (2005): 77–91.

Mühl, Johannes C. M. "Empirical Validation of the Lovemarks Concept —A Structural Equation Study." Diss. University of Mannheim, 2009. Web. 5 Aug 2009.

Nobre, Helen. "Should Consumers Be in Love With Brands? An Investigation Into the Influence That Specific Consumer–Brand Relationships Have on the Quality of the Bonds That Consumers Develop With Brands." *Journal of Transnational Management* 16.4 (2011): 270–281.

Percy, Larry. "Understanding the Role of Emotion in Advertising." Copenhagen Business School, 2003. Web. 10 Oct 2009.

Sarkar, Abhigyan. "Loving a Brand: Empirical Investigation of Consumer–Brand Love Relationship." *International Journal of Applied Behavioral Economics* 1.3 (2012): 28–38.

Credits

Cover
Saatchi & Saatchi Design
Worldwide, Auckland,
New Zealand, Designer Kane
McPherson, Creative Director
Blake Enting

Foreword
p7: Photographer Kate Ayrton,
Source www.saatchikevin.com

**Case Stories Double-Page
Spread**
p10 (first row, left) The Ritz-
Carlton: Team One
Los Angeles, USA,
Photographer Geof Kern,
Photographer Eric Schwabel;
Rylie Martinez (child) – Talent
Agency Ford Models, Amber
Rivera (mom) – Talent Agency
cesd; Bianca Palmerin Talent
Agency Wilhelmina

p10 (first row, right) SKOL:
F/Nazca Saatchi & Saatchi
Brazil, Bullet, Photographer
Rodrigo Netto

p10 (second row, right) Toyota
Camry: Saatchi & Saatchi Los
Angeles, USA, Photographer
Ryley Brown

p10 (third row left) Cheerios:
Saatchi & Saatchi New York,
USA, Photographers Jenn
Ackerman and Tim Gruber,
Ackerman + Gruber

p10 (third row, right)
T-Mobile: Saatchi & Saatchi
London, UK, Director Michael
Gracey, Production Company
Partizan

p11 (first row, left) Lenovo:
Saatchi & Saatchi New York,
USA

p11 (first row, middle)
Guinness: Saatchi & Saatchi
South Africa

p11 (first row, right) Miller
High Life: Saatchi & Saatchi
New York, USA, Actor Windell
Middlebrooks

p11 (second row, left) Lexus:
Team One Los Angeles,
USA, Director Gary Johns,
Production Company
Johns+Gorman Films

p11 (second row, middle) Nike:
F/Nazca Saatchi & Saatchi
Brazil

p11 (second row, right) Visa:
Saatchi & Saatchi London,
UK, Director Joey Garfield,
Production Company
Academy

p11 (third row, left) BGH:
F/Nazca Saatchi & Saatchi
Brazil, Director Diego y Vlady,
Production Company Peluca
Films

p11 (third row, center, upper
image) Safeguard: Saatchi &
Saatchi China, Director Shen
Yan, Production Company
GZ Only Production, Actor Li
Wan Feng

p11 (third row, center, lower
image) Blood Relations: BBR
Saatchi & Saatchi Israel

Chapter 01 – Lovemarks
p15: Centrade Saatchi &
Saatchi, Romania Creative
Director Johan Ohlson
Creative Group Head Laura
Iane Art Director Bogdan
Vintila, Copywriter Andrei
Nica, Senior Account
Manager Ioana Hurdubelea,
Sr. Account Executive
Madalina Floria, Account
Executive Cristina Alexandru,
Prepress Manager Dan Butoi,
Corporate Communication
Manager Corina Pisc

p19: Saatchi & Saatchi Design
Worldwide, Auckland, New
Zealand, Designers Kane
McPherson and Josephine
Ross

p22, 23: Saatchi & Saatchi X,
Springdale, Arkansas USA,
Photographer Stewart Cohen

Chapter 02 – Xploring
p27, 29, 32, 33, 34, 35, 36:
Saatchi & Saatchi London,
UK and Saatchi & Saatchi
South Africa

p39: Saatchi & Saatchi China

Chapter 03 – People Power
p43, 50: Photographer Ryley
Brown

p45, 46, 49: Saatchi & Saatchi
Los Angeles, USA

p53, 54: F/Nazca Saatchi &
Saatchi Brazil, Photographer
Rodrigo Netto

p55: F/Nazca Saatchi &
Saatchi Brazil

Chapter 04 – Tribes
p59, 68: Saatchi & Saatchi
New York, USA,
Photographers Jenn
Ackerman and Tim Gruber,
Ackerman + Gruber

p61: Saatchi & Saatchi
New York, USA and
Saatchi & Saatchi London, UK

p62, 63: Saatchi & Saatchi
New York, USA and Saatchi &
Saatchi London, UK, Director
Jan Gleie, Production
Company Twin Film Munich

p66: Saatchi & Saatchi
New York, USA

p67: Saatchi & Saatchi
New York, USA, Photographer
Daniella Perez

Chapter 05 – Virality
p73, 74, 78, 80: Saatchi &
Saatchi London, UK, Director
Michael Gracey, Production
Company Partizan

p86, 87: Saatchi & Saatchi
Fallon Tokyo, Japan

Chapter 06 – Rallying Cries
p91, 95, 99, 100: Saatchi &
Saatchi New York, USA

p92: Saatchi & Saatchi
New York, USA, Arrechedera
Claverol Mexico, Photographer
Gabriel Chouy

p97: Lenovo Photo Library,
Flickr

p100: Saatchi & Saatchi
New York, USA, Photographer
Danny Clinch

Credits cont.

Acknowledgements

I would like to thank all of the following people who helped in ways big and small, and without whom this project could never have succeeded.

Adrian Farina
Agustina Calcagno
Alaina Lovera
Alan Hallberg
Amy Martin
Andrea Mendelevich
Andrew Tunnicliffe
Andy Bell
Ann Jingco
Augustina Del Campo
Aziz Jindani
Ben Court
Betsy Reithemeyer
Bianca Hertel
Bill Cochrane
Bob Zeinstra
Blake Enting
Brandon McGraw
Brendan Noonan
Brian Carley
Brian Sweeney
Carla Hofler
Carly Wallace
Carmen Rodriguez
Charlie Finnigan
Charlotte Grey
Chris Gabaldon
Chuck Maguy
Claudine Cheever
Cliff Francis
Connor Bryant
Daniella Perez
Deb Henretta
Debbie Carberry

Deborah Mills
Derek Lockwood
Dieter Haberl
Doug Van Andel
Emily Deutsch
Eric Ern
Evan Ferrari
Ezequiel Devoto
Fabio Fernandes
Flora Proverbio
Graham Cruikshanks
Guilherme Glezer
Gus Marmarinos
Hank Sheehan
Heidi Young
Herve Humler
Hosanna Marshall
James Barker
James Tsao
Jane Wagner
Janet Allgaier
Jason Levine
Jason Lonsdale
Jeremy Macey
Jerry Beers
Jodi Allen
Joe Abegg
John Brase
John Dunleavy
Jose Porto
Josephine Ross
Julie Michael
Kane McPherson
Kate Sheehan

Kate Stanners
Kathryn Neugold
Katie Moore
Kejal Crosson-Elturan
Kelly Engstrom
Kevin O'Neill
Kevin Roberts
Laura Mills
Laura Pacas
Laura Xiong
Linda Bennett
Lisa Matthews
Lorraine Branham
Maria Sheehan
Mariano Dima
Marc Pritchard
Mark Cochrane
Mark Miller
Mark Rolland
Mark Templin
Mark Turner
Mary Ann Contartesi
Martin Riant
Maru Kopelowicz
Mary Baglivo
Meghan Sturges
Michael Rebelo
Michelle Greenhalgh
Murray Streets
Neal Fairfield
Neel Chaurasia
Nick Miaritis
Nick Teare
Nicole LaValette

Nilla Sheehan
Pablo Del Campo
Paul Mareski
Paul Silburn
Pedro Earp
Peter Moore Smith
Phil Rubel
Rachael Jackman
Rachel Macbeth
Rebecca Lee
Richard Huntington
Richard Hytner
Rieko Aiba
Robert Senior
Rodes Ponzer
Ruairi Twomey
Sarah Tan
Scott Geraghty
Scott Gilbert
Scott Schreiber
Scott Thompson
Shand Spencer
Sona Iliffe-Moon
Sophie Mills
Stacey Noyle
Stephen Hanselman
Steve Rothman
Steven Chan
Susie Kamm
Tamara Lover
Thierry Ibri
Tim Morrison
Vaughan Emsley
Yossi Lubaton

Loveworks

How the world's top marketers
make emotional connections
to win in the marketplace

Text © 2013 Brian Sheehan

Foreword © 2013 Kevin Roberts

All images used with permission and © their respective owners.

All rights reserved. No part of this book may be reproduced in any manner in
any media, or transmitted by any means whatsoever, electronic or mechanical
(including photocopy, film or video, Internet posting, or any other information
storage and retrieval system) without prior written permission.

Published in the United States by powerHouse Books,
a division of powerHouse Cultural Entertainment, Inc.
37 Main Street, Brooklyn, NY 11201-1021
telephone 212 604 9074
e-mail: info@powerHouseBooks.com
website: www.powerHouseBooks.com

First edition, 2013

Library of Congress Control Number: 2012955755

Hardcover ISBN 978-1-57687-640-4

Art Direction and Design:
Kane McPherson, Saatchi & Saatchi Design Worldwide

Printed and bound in China through Asia Pacific Offset

10 9 8 7 6 5 4 3 2 1